# NATURE OF RELIGIOUS BELIEF:
# THE LINGUISTIC APPROACH

# Nature of Religious Belief: The Linguistic Approach

**K.N. Tiwari**

MOTILAL BANARSIDASS
INTERNATIONAL
DELHI

First Edition : Delhi, 2026

© Author

ISBN : 978-81-19394-44-9

*Also available at*
MOTILAL BANARSIDASS INTERNATIONAL
H.O. : 41 U.A. Bungalow Road, (Back Lane)Jawahar Nagar, Delhi - 110 007
4261 (basement) Lane #3,Ansari Road, Darya Ganj, New Delhi - 110 002
Shop No. 6, Luz Ginza Complex, 241 Luz Corner, Mylapore, Chennai - 600 004
12/1A, 2nd Floor, Bankim Chatterjee Street, Kolkata - 700 073
*Stockist* : Motilal Books, Ashok Rajpath, Near Kali Mandir, Patna - 800 004

No part of this book may be reproduced in any form or by any electronic or mechanical means including information storage and retrieval systems without permission in writing from the publishers, excepts by a reviewer who may quote brief passages in a review.

Printed in India
MOTILAL BANARSIDASS INTERNATIONAL

# CONTENTS

*Introduction* .................................................................. vii

1. Language-Analysis and Philosophy .............................. 1
2. Defence of the Factual Nature of Religious Belief ..... 8
   *Section I: Verifiability* ................................................. 8
   i. Introductory ....................................................... 8
   ii. Appeal to Religious Experience ........................ 9
   iii. A Critical Estimate ............................................ 17
   *Section II: Proofs for the Existence of God* ................ 29
   i. The Proofs .......................................................... 30
   ii. Conclusion ......................................................... 69
   *Section III: Faith* ......................................................... 77
   *Section IV: Attributes of God and the Question of Factuality of Religious Belief* ............ 88
   i. Scepticism about the Factual Nature of the Attributes ................................................ 90
   ii. A Defence (By an Appeal to Analogical or Metaphorical Predication) ......................... 104
   iii. An Estimate ....................................................... 111
3. Opposition (Refutation) of the Factual Nature of Religious Belief: Falsifiability ............................... 119
   i. Principle of Falsifiability and the Status of Religious Belief ............................................ 120
   ii. Falsifiability and a Defence of the Factuality of Religious Belief ............................ 125

4. **Non-Factual Analyses of the Nature of Religious Belief** .......................................................... 140
   i. Religious Statements as Emotive .......................... 141
   ii. Religious Statements as Statements of 'Confession', 'Conversion', 'A Free Decision Made in Faith and Love' .......... 144
   iii. Religious Statements as Volitional or Moral ...... 148
   iv. Religious Statements as Evocative of All-pervasive Dispositions—Mental, Physical and Emotional ......................................... 156
   v. Religious Statements as 'Blik'-statements ........... 169

5. **True Nature of Religious Belief— Author's View** .................................................................. 177

6. **Concluding Observations** ............................................ 206

*Bibliography* ............................................................................. 213

# INTRODUCTION

Our chief concern in this book has been to analyse the nature of religious belief with a view to understanding its true nature. The term 'religious belief' includes within it some or all of the following beliefs—belief in God, belief in the immortality of soul, belief in an after-life, belief in heaven and hell, and so on. But here we have used the term only in the first sense, i.e., in the sense of belief in God and have tried to see what this believing in God actually means and implies. Ordinarily speaking, believing in God means believing in the existence of an objective reality having various metaphysical and ethical attributes. But our aim here has been to see how far this sense of the nature of belief in God is true and with what implications.

The question 'what does believing in God actually imply?' may be dealt with in more than one way. But we have adopted here the method of language-analysis, i.e. the method of the analysis of concepts and statements related to God-belief, for dealing with the question. But the question here is how to carry on this analysis of religious language so that the real nature of religious belief may come out before us. It is quite well known by now that from some time back the role of philosophy has more been analysis of language and search for it's real meaning rather than search for truth and reality. But the job of analysis of language hence search for it's real meaning has not been an arbitrary job rather various principles and theories have been developed in the light of which the job of analysis and search for meaning are to be carried On.

It is by keeping in view these logical principles, theories and criteria that the job of analysis, all religious language especially of religious statements has been carried on so as to reach the real nature of religious belief. A brief picture of the principles and theories developed for the of language analysis has been drawn in chapter one.

Recent analyses of God-statements have generally assumed two forms which may be called (1) factual or cognitive and (2) non-factual or non-cognitive. The first kind of analysis has aimed at showing that religious statements refer to and describe a personal being who, although infinite in nature, is still real and objective. Religious statements, therefore, although referring to a unique kind of reality, are still factual or cognitive in nature in the same sense, though not in the same way, in which our ordinary factual or scientific statements are so. The second kind of analysis, on the other hand, has aimed at showing that religious statements have got no referential import and their apparent factual or cognitive nature is simply deceptive.

They are therefore to be understood in a different light in accordance with the actual job they are used to perform. Different thinkers, however, have taken this job performed by the religious statements differently. Some have taken religious statements being used for expressing the deep passion of the religious believers, others have taken them as expressing the intentions of the believers to behave in a particular way, still others have taken them as expressing or evoking all-pervasive patterns of behaviour, and so on.

We have taken the view that both the kinds of analyses are one-sided. None of them is true to the actual use of these statements as made by the religious believers. In the religious man's use or assertion of religious statements we may very well mark two important points—(1) He asserts these statements as factual statements and also seems to mean them as such, (2) He asserts them with a sense of commitment such that in no conceivable situation he would be ready to hold them false. Any true analysis of religious statements must take care of both these features of the religious man's assertion of his statements. The first kind of analysis takes care of the first feature but neglects the second one. Similarly, the second takes care of the second feature but neglects the first one. Hence both are one-sided. No analysis of religious belief will be true to its nature unless the analysis is made by keeping it close to the way or ways the religious believer asserts his belief through his various statements. We have felt therefore that a correct analysis of the nature of religious belief consists in a golden mean between the two typical trends of analyses that we have hinted at above. And that is what we have attempted in our last chapter to do. The analysis, to our mind, does ample justice to both the features of religious man's assertion of his belief as noted above and therefore it presents the true nature of religious belief.

On the basis of our analysis, we have also tried to derive certain far-reaching conclusions regarding the nature of religious experience etc. We have come to the conclusion that the basic religious experience is of somewhat a pantheistic nature and theism is an after-product of human act of symbolization. In this respect we have upheld the veracity of the basic position of *Samkara*, the great *Vedantin*, according to whom an all-pervasive *Brahman* is the fundamental reality and God is merely an expedient or useful symbol to help man realize the ultimate reality or *Brahman*. A nearly similar position has been taken by Paul Tillich also when he takes Being-itself to be the fundamental reality and God merely a symbol.

We have also tried to define religion in our own way on the basis of our analysis of the nature of religious belief. We have been able in our opinion to find a definition which is equally applicable to theistic and non-theistic religions, although we have arrived at it on the basis of an analysis of what may properly be called theistic belief.

# 1
# LANGUAGE-ANALYSIS AND PHILOSOPHY

Traditionally philosophy as a study has been a search after the nature of the fundamental reality or truth. In this search, although experience of whatever is there before us outside and within has played an important role, but, the main instrument has been speculation. This may not be taken as literally true about Indian philosophy, but here we will be mainly talking about western philosophy. Philosophers in their effort to make search after Truth on the basis of speculation have actually been able to erect lofty edifices about the nature, structure, number etc. of the fundamental truth or reality in their own different ways. Understood in a different way their effort has resulted in a kind of lofty system-building depicting the nature of reality and its several possible ramifications and manifestations explaining the cosmos and its different aspects. This kind of system-building went on and on at the hands of coming philosophers until it seemed to culminate in what is called the philosophy of Absolute Idealism. Beginning from Hegel and proceeding ahead through the latter Absolute idealists like Bradley and Bosanquet, very attractive and lofty edifices regarding the nature etc. of Reality was erected. But such kind of edifices invited reactions complaining that these were all juggalries of vague and mystified expressions which made nothing clear about the nature of Reality. Reactions came in the form of certain concrete philosophies like Pragmatism, Realism, Logical positivism and philosophy of linguistic analysis and Existentialism, of these, logical positivism and philosophy of language-analysis played a very crucial and formidable role in as much as they actually changed the very nature and goal of philosophical thinking.

It was felt by many thinkers that because philosophy after centuries of speculative research has been able to yield nothing other than some lofty structures in vague and mystified words and expressions or attractive system depicting the nature and structure of reality like beautiful castles in the air, what was needed most was the classification of the meaning of language through which things about reality or truth where claimed to be brought about. So henceforth in a way the new goal or nature of philosophy was taken to be the analysis of language, so that things said vaguely in a large sound and mystery should be made clear. Instead of making philosophy a field for the searching after the nature of reality , analysis of language should be made the very nature and goal of philosophy.

At the first instance philosopher instead of making a neutral analysis of the language of philosophy specifically of what is generally called metaphysics, took a very drastic step of distinguishing between meaningful and meaningless language on the basis of a criterion of meaningfulness. Such philosophers were specifically called philosophers of Vienna circle or more particularly logical positivists. The theory of meaning that they propounded was known as verifiability theory of meaning, according to which any statement to be meaningful must have to be verified with reference to some sense experience. They actually had a pre-planned idea to develop some such criterion of meaning which could declare all statements of metaphysics, religions, ethics etc. as meaningless. The above criterion gave them a full of opportunity to declare such statements as meaningless. Because according to them after so many years of speculation nothing meaningful about reality or truth could be ascertained, it was better to declare all statements related to this kind of research as meaningless.

But the way in which all metaphysical and religious statements were declared meaningless in one stroke on the strength of an arbitrary theory of meaning was not approved by all. Logical positivist where mainly based on logical atomism, philosophy developed mainly on the basis of a book *Tractatus-Logico-Philosophicus* written by Wittgenstein, although it was fully developed by Russell. In due course Wittgenstein himself did not agree with the views he expressed in *Tractatus* and wrote another famous book *Philosophical Investigations* which is really the mother of all subsequent language analysis in philosophy whether it be in the sphere of metaphysics or religion or ethics or some other discipline such as law history etc.

I shall not go here into the details of the ideas of language and its meaning developed or propounded in the light of *Philosophical Investigation*, but simply point out to some very popular and which really governed, guided and directed all subsequent analysis of language of any discipline or branch office study. The slogans: (1) Don't look for meaning, look for use, (2) No language or statement is meaningless; every statement has its logic and that has to be found out by a proper analysis of language, (3) There may be a distinction between the apparent logic (meaning) and real logic of a statement and that has to be found out by a proper and piecemeal analysis of any language or statement. The first slogan actually counsels that language has a variety of uses and in all its uses it has meaning, thought of different types. Therefore we have not to look for in case if any language whether it has meaning or not, or, in other words, whether it is meaningful or meaningless. And the meaning of any language or statement has to be ascertained by looking to the different kinds of uses to which it is put. That will give us an idea of what is the real meaning of a word in the different context, in which it is used. That will give us a clear understanding of how it is to be used in language. Second and the third taken together employ that no language or statement is meaningless. It has some or other of meaning. Maybe what seems apparently to be its meaning is not actually it's real meaning, the actual meaning is something else which has to be found out from an analysis of the apparent meaning.

Of the variety of languages expressing variety of things, we are concerned here mainly with religious language. But religious language itself has various aspects or dimensions it may be about heaven and hell it may be about redemption and liberation Verma it may be about soul and other spiritual beings, it may be about life after death and so on. But the most important kind of religious language is that which is concerned about the experience of God and the various properties given to him. This part of religious language is generally of the subject-object form the subject referring to some objective reality generally called God and the predicate describing the nature and characteristics of God. This part of religious language is generally given the name of 'religious statement'. We shall be mainly concerned here with the nature of these statements, because our aim here is to try to ascertain the exact nature of religious belief. Religious belief as a matter of fact includes many kind of beliefs, but here we will confine ourselves to what we may call belief in God—the believe that God exists, possess such and such properties, has created the world and does also sustain and maintain it etc. etc. The main problems about these statements is that apparently they look like factual statements referring to an objective reality called God and the predicates describing him. Are they actually so ? In other words, is the real meaning of these statements also the same as their apparent meaning? The whole nature of religious belief in the sense of God-belief depends upon the answer to this question. If the answer is 'yes', that, is if the answer is that the real meaning of these statements is exactly the same as their apparent meaning, then having religious belief will imply the believers' positive acceptance that there is a God behind or beneath the world which is created by him. The way the believer utter their statements corroborates his belief in the reality of a God. His religious behaviour also collaborate with his above belief. If the answer however is 'no' then we have to search after the real meaning of these statements by a proper analysis of the meaning of the term and concepts used in them. But how do this work of analysis of terms and concepts so that the real nature of these statements may come out before us?

In recent times a very useful criterion has been developed by some logicians and philosophers of science such as by Karl popper, which will ascertain decisively whether a statement is factual or not, or in other words, whether it has got a factual meaning or not. We shall discuss this criterion in due course and see its implication in case of religious statements. But before that we will like to see the efforts of some of theological thinkers who, in spite of all hurdles and objections, have tried to show in their own ways that the so called apparent meaning of religious statement is also their real meaning.

The first effort in this direction is made by thinkers like A. C. Ewind, S. D. Lewis etc. who take up the case of factuality of religious statements head on against the verificationist who insist that a statement has meaning or at least a factual meaning, if and only if it is verifiable with reference to some experience or more particularly with some sense experience. The second effort is made by advancing various proofs for the existence of God such that the objectivity of the subject term 'God' of religious statements may be established and the factuality of religious statement may be reasserted. Actually these proofs have been advanced traditionally also but recently in the light of the analytic movement in philosophy, they have been advanced in fresh manner and the assessment thereof also have been done in an analytical way in the light of the linguistic movement in philosophy. The third effort has been made in terms of faith. Comparing the situation of faith with that of ordinary knowledge, faith has been given the status of knowledge and on the strength of that the factuality of religious statement has been tried to be established. Then finally, the predicate have been analysed and it has been tried to show that they have genuine predicates describing an objective reality in the subject. All these efforts we will see in the next chapter and after making this critical assessment we shall try to see the implications of recently developed falsification theory of factual meaning. Falsifiability has proved to be decisive yardstick for fixing whether a statement is factual or not. On this yardstick religious statements have been finally proved not to be factual

But we have seen that any statement not being factual, although it looks like that, does not mean that it has no meaning. Its apparent meaning may be deceptive, but it has some real meaning and that has to be found out. Many thinkers who have been totally under the influence of falsifiability theory have taken them finally as non-factual and have engaged themselves in giving different types of meaning to the religious statements. Thinkers like Stevenson, Ayer, Braithwaite, Schmidt, etc. have fully applied themselves towards suggesting the real meaning of the religious statements hidden behind there apparent meaning. How far there suggestions stand up to the demands of the religious statements as understood by the religious believers will have to be assessed and that has been done. Even accepted that religious statements are not factual, any kind of improvisation or presumption will not do. While trying to understand the real meaning of any language, I think the users of the language must have to be taken into confidence. No language can mean anything by keeping them complete apart from their users. And that is equally true of religious language or religious statement also. The author has actually made in effort to think in this direction so that the nature of religious belief maybe deciphered through the language the believer utters to express the kind of belief he entertains within him while expressing the belief in language. While doing this again, it will have to be kept in mind that by the final suggestion that is made neither the internal religious experience of the believer is not given due importance, nor the principles of valid logic are blatantly ignored.

# 2

# DEFENCE OF THE FACTUAL NATURE OF RELIGIOUS BELIEF

## SECTION I
## VERIFIABILITY

### i. Introductory

We have seen that the logical positivists tried to refute metaphysical and religious beliefs as absolutely insignificant and nonsense on the basis of a criterion of meaningfulness propounded in the form of verifiability theory. In general outlines, the theory demanded that any belief to be meaningful must be capable of verification with reference to some sense-experience.

Now, as a criterion of meaningfulness, we have seen, the theory could not stand long, but as a criterion of 'factual' meaningfulness the theory still has some force and has important bearings all beliefs or statements which claim to be factual or cognitive. Religious beliefs also, we find, claim to be factual and theologians who favour such a claim of these beliefs have not been deaf and unresponsive to the relevant force of the verifiability demand. They have really faced the challenge from the verifiability demand head on and have tried to show in face of that, that religious beliefs also, like ordinary factual or scientific beliefs, have got some empirical basis, some empirical evidences behind them so that their truth or falsity can be ascertained with reference to them. Some have taken the challenge from the verifiability criterion so directly that they have really made attempts to show that just as in the case of scientific beliefs there are sense-empirical evidences, similarly in the case of religious beliefs also there are such evidences. The presence of the causal law although the world, the existence of system and order everywhere are some of the clear sense-empirical evidences which speak of the existence of a God behind the world. Belief in God is amply justified with reference to sense-empirical data present in the world. F.R. Tennant has been one very important contemporary thinker to preach such a view.[1] But such pleas to defend the factual or empirical nature of religious beliefs can hardly be supported. Such empirical justifications of religious beliefs made by Tennant and others are really nothing different from showing the validity of the causal and teleological arguments for the existence of God. And these arguments, it is well established now, do not constitute valid proofs for the existence of God.

## ii. Appeal to Religious Experience

The defence that has more often been brought about of religious beliefs in terms of verifiability is that they are, like ordinary factual beliefs, verifiable with reference to an experience, but such an experience is not, and can never be, sense-experience. Religious beliefs, by their very nature, purport to be beliefs about a fact (or facts) which transcends (or transcend) sense-experience. And hence it is absurd to seek a verification of them by sense-experience. Sense-experience is not the only experience that man has and therefore to confine the use of the word 'experience' in such a way exhibits nothing but a sense of dogmatism, narrowness, arbitrariness and a pre-possessed bias on the part of the positivists. By this act of narrowness, the positivists leave a vast track of human experience untrodden, exclude from consideration great tracts of reality and confine themselves within a constricted. and impoverished world."[2]

The experience to which religious statements are to be referred for their empirical verification is known as 'religious experience'. With certain minor differences, the experience is also known as mystical experience, or intuitive experience, or personal encounter, spiritual vision etc. Therefore, whatever we will say about religious experience will, more or less, also apply to all these. Amongst contemporary thinkers, those who have tried to save the factual and cognitive status of religious beliefs or statements by referring them to religious experiences, the names of H.D. Lewis, John Wilson, A.C. Ewing, etc. are leading. It is not a fact that all of these thinkers make an appeal to religious experience exactly in the same way to defend the factual status of religious statements, nevertheless, all of them somehow try to establish that religious beliefs are not emotive, psychological or some thing like that. They try to establish by reference to religious experience that they have some objective content and they refer to some objective, real situation. Such objective facts or situations (with reference to which the truth or falsity of the religious statements is to be verified are somehow revealed to us in some unique kind of experience known as religious experience. These experiences, although occurring to only a few, are still genuine experiences and are experiences of something perfectly real and objective. They are not mere subjective fancies or certain subjective states of feelings or emotions, as some contemporary empirical thinkers take them to be. Religious statements, there-fore, are not merely emotive or expressive in character; they and informative. refer to objective facts and therefore they are factual cognitive

Now, the above view that religious statements have an objective referent clearly means that God exists as an objective reality. Here again, all of the above thinkers agree on the point that although God exists objectively, his existence is in no way comparable to the existence of ordinary physical objects. He does not exist in the fashion of a table's or chair's existence. God exists in his own unique way and his existence and nature although revealed to us to some extent in religious experiences, remain, for the most part, a 'mystery'. But again, they emphasize, that on that account, i.e., on account of the fact that God's being is a mystery, we cannot say that there is nothing like true or false about the religious beliefs, that they do not refer to any objective situation. Because God is a mystery, religious statements are naturally metaphorical but their metaphorical nature does not prevent them from being factual and cognitive. The logic of religious statements is not basically different from that of ordinary factual statements.

Now, as we have said, although the various thinkers named above agree on these essential points, they differ as to their detailed approach and treatment of the matter. To see the point of each, let us have a brief consideration of their views separately. Amongst all the thinkers Lewis seems to be the most enthusiastic to save the factual and cognitive status of religious beliefs. He insists more than once that religious statements have an objective content, they refer to a 'beyond' and that the questions of truth and falsity must somehow be applicable to them in the literal sense.[3] "A religion must stand the test of truth and falsity in the normal sense ... there must be at the core of religion something significant to which the distinction of true and false in the normal or literal sense applies."[4] In contemporary philosophical theology there are two kinds of views as to the nature of religious statements: (1) Religious statements are not factual. Their direct indicative forms are logically misleading. They are to be interpreted indirectly, in an oblique way. (2) Religious statements are factual, but they are so in their own ways. They have a private, autonomous status, and the questions of truth and falsity in the ordinary sense are inapplicable to them. Lewis opposes both these views and strongly holds that religious statements are factual and cognitive and the considerations of truth and falsity must be applied to them in the literal, normal sense. Logically, religious language is not different from ordinary factual language. And just as the question of truth and falsity of ordinary factual statements is decided with reference to sense-experience, similarly the question of the truth and falsity of religious statements is to be ascertained with reference to religious experience.

But all this does not mean that God exists exactly in the same way in which the ordinary physical objects exist. Again, it does not mean that God is revealed in our religious experiences in a 'total' way. The nature and existence of God, for the most, remain a mystery to us and this mystery can never be unveiled in totto. It is really this element of mystery which is the corner-stone of religion. Lewis much emphasizes this element of mystery[5] in relation to the object of religion and points out in consequence that religious experiences are also for the most part elusive and mysterious. Lewis criticises such a view of religious experience which tells of a direct 'I-thou encounter where the soul or the individual is in a direct, face-to-face, relationship with God so as to have a total apprehension of him. Total or complete apprehension of God is never possible. The notion of a direct 'I-thou' encounter is a misrepresentation of the true nature of the experience of God. The mystery around God always eludes our total apprehension of him. Now, because religious experiences are elusive and mysterious, it is natural that religious statements will be elusive and metaphorical. But this, says Lewis, is a false prejudice to assume that the elusive or metaphorical nature of religious statements debars them from all considerations of truth and falsity. Every religious experience inspite of being mysterious has an element of cognition in it and this cognition has an element of certainty in it as compelling as that found in logic and mathematics. "It must be stressed, however, that the elusive insight or intuition in question has the same compelling character as the apprehensions we have in logic and mathematics. It presents what we feel must be the case, and its elusiveness in other regards does not affect the certainty it brings."[6] Religious experience reveals the mystery of religion to us to some extent and to the extent it does so we can very well use religious language cognitively.

Like Lewis, John Wilson is also very enthusiastic about defending the factual status of religious statements by an appeal to religious experience. He is rather even more insistent and forceful in his language to establish that religious statements are as much factual assertions as our ordinary empirical statements are and that God is as much objective a reality or fact as our ordinary sense-objects are. He, of course, recognises that God does not exist in the same way as a table or chair exists. He asserts that the way in which God exists is, for the most part, a mystery, and that he cannot be so easily apprehended as ordinary objects are done, but still God is objective and the statements about him are genuinely factual and informative. As is clear from his unambiguous statement: "To say 'there is a God' is to state a fact: God is real in the same sense, though not in the same way, as physical objects are real ..."[7] The word 'God', therefore, refers to a perfectly objective reality according to Wilson and that statements about God are all genuine assertions expressing that such and such is the case and such is not the case. They are thus capable of being verified and falsified and are, therefore, to be put "in the same logical boat, as it were, with straightforward empirical statements."[8]

Now, the question arises, how is the factual, informative status of the religious statements to be justified? That is, in other words, how are they to be verified? For a statement to be factual and informative and to be put in the same logical boat as that of the ordinary empirical statements, we have seen, it is necessary that it is verifiable and falsifiable with reference to some experience. Now, if religious statements claim to be as much factual, cognitive and informative as the straightforward empirical statements, how are they verified? Wilson's brief answer to this question is "By religious experience". As he himself puts the matter: "How are religious statements ultimately verified? Briefly, my answer will be, "By religious experience."[9] Wilson criticises the notion of verifiability with reference to sense-experience merely[10] and points out that there is no valid logical ground to limit the word 'experience" within the narrow boundary of 'sense-experience' merely.[1] Each statement must be sought to be tested with reference to an experience which is suited to or is in consonance with the nature of the assertion. As Wilson himself says: " ... assertions do have to pass tests, not arbitrary tests, but tests which they impose on themselves, as it were, because of what they assert."[11]

In spite of the force with which Wilson tries to establish that God is real and that the statements about God are cognitive, factual and informative, he is not prepared to say, as we have seen above, that God is a reality, an object just like a table or a chair. We have seen him saying above that God is real in the same *sense*, but not in the same way as the physical objects are. He is prepared to accept, like Lewis, that for the most part God is a mystery and to a great extent his nature is uncomprehended.[12] But then this mysterious nature, according to him, does not prevent us from cognising and saying at least something about him. In our future experiences, we may be able to know more and more about God, and accordingly, we can go on extending the meaning of the word 'God'. There is nothing in logic to prevent it. As he says: "Instead of Vedantist's 'Not this, not this', Christians must be able to say, 'At least this, at least this'. They must be able to assert definitely about God, whilst admitting that there is far more to be known about Him than we can perhaps ever hope to know. Moreover, as we come to learn more about God, there is nothing in logic to prevent our expanding the meaning of the word 'God'".[13] Moreover, Wilson also admits that much of religious language is metaphorical, but metaphors, according to him are not vacuous, "because a metaphor may assert something quite as precise and informative as any other assertion."[14]

In the chain of the thinkers who have tried to defend the cognitive status of religious statements by defending their verifiability with reference to religious experiences, A.C. Ewing also does not lag behind. In one of his essays,[15] Ewing has strongly defended the genuineness of intuitive or religious experiences as being perfectly objective and cognitive in nature. His main argument here in face of the criticisms of religious experience made by the positivists seems to be that if the genuineness of such experiences as being objective and cognitive cannot be conclusively established, it cannot be conclusively refuted either. If no conclusive proofs can be advanced in support of the claim of the mystic that he is having the experience of God, no good reasons can either be given to prove that his contention is wrong.

And so, according to Ewing, "... there are certain 'mystical' and other religious experiences which can without argument adequately and rationally assure one of God's existence."[16] Those who dispute the genuineness of such experiences as being perfectly cognitive in nature are, according to Ewing, like those 'tone-deaf' men who are unable to hear and recognise the value of Beethoven's music. If sense-experience can be believed as giving us genuine factual and cognitive information, why not religious experience, "why should 'facts' be necessarily limited to those potentially present to sense-perception?"[17]

"In every cognition", says Ewing, "there is an inference from experience to object. "[18] Now if such an inference is warranted and justified in case of our ordinary cognitions, why should the same be taken unwarranted and unjustified in case of religious cognitions? It is on such arguments that Ewing tries to defend the factual and cognitive status of religious statements.

Besides the thinkers mentioned above, Basil Mitchell and Ian Ramsey may also be mentioned in this chain, but we are leaving them out here for certain reasons. Basil Mitchell tries to defend the factual status of religious statements by an appeal to religious experience in his essay 'The Grace of God'.[19] In this essay Mitchell specifically deals with the factual nature of one's belief in the grace of God, but by implication, he talks about religious beliefs in general too. But still, we are missing a detailed consideration of his views here, because his views in the essay raise certain problems of such a specific nature which will make us deviate from the general trend of our discussion which is relevant to our aim here. Ramsey's analysis baffles our understanding in as much as it does not seem clear to us whether he is for defending the genuine factual status of religious statements like those whom we have dealt with above or he stands on a different ground. Of course, his emphasis at times on the objectivity of the religious situation makes one thing that he is defending the factual status of religious statements. But still so far as we have understood him, as he stands in his book,

'*Religious Language*'[20], it seems that he is not defending the factual status of religious statements in a manner and with a tone with which the above thinkers do so. At least, he is not anxious to assimilate these statements with the scientific ones. We, therefore, reserve the consideration of his views for some other place where, we think, it will be more appropriate.

### iii. A Critical Estimate

We have seen above some of the important attempts to defend the objective, factual or cognitive status of religious statements by an appeal to religious experience. In all such attempts, it is clear, what the defenders want to show is that religious statements are certainly not scientific statements, because the former are not verifiable like the latter with reference to sense-experience. Nevertheless, religious statements are like scientific statements, have an objective, factual status similar to that of the scientific statements, because just as the latter refer to, describe, and are verifiable with reference to the facts of sense-experience, the former also refer to, describe, and are verifiable with reference to a perfectly objective fact revealed to us in our religious experience. Now, as we have said already earlier, there is *prima facie* no wrong with such a claim. But the point is that, if religious statements claim to stand at a par with the scientific statements then the former also must have to be verifiable with reference to religious. experience in the same way as the latter are verifiable with reference to sense-experience. Now, scientific statements are verifiable with reference to sense-experience in a *public* manner. That the sense-experience with reference to which a particular scientific statement is to be verified is not confined to only one or two persons, but it is open to all those whose senses are in order, and each one can repeat his experience as many times as he wills so as to confirm the result of his verification. Thus, in case of scientific statements there are repeatable public checking procedures. Are there such public verifications or public checking-procedures possible in case of religious statements?

Certainly not. Religious experiences are rare. They occur to only a few and that also on certain special moments. Such experiences are not open to all, and in case of those also who have such experiences, they are not repeatable at will. How can then religious statements claim the same objective or factual status as that of the scientific statements?

Wilson, however, seems fully alive to the above difficulties in the path of the objectivity or genuine cognitivity of the religious statements. He distinguishes between objective and subjective, existential and psychological statements by pointing out that while the former are concerned with a matter of public interest, the latter are not so. Distinguishing the two modes of statement, he himself says, "The former are concerned with matter of public interest and experience to a degree that the latter are not."[21] And again, "We use the two modes of speech, existential and psychological, precisely because we wish to distinguish matters which are of public interest from matters which are not: to distinguish autobiographical remarks from common facts."[22] But again, on the basis of these distinctions, Wilson does not give up the objectivity of religious statements, rather he argues for their objective and existential status on the plea that they are also matters of public interest and experience. Of course, the word 'public', Wilson concedes, is not to be taken here in the same broad sense in which we take it in case of scientific statements. The word 'public' means here a group—a large group—the group of the religious persons. Within such a religious group, religious statements are publicly verifiable. Such religious people, Wilson says, have not only common, but co-recurrent religious experiences and such experiences can even be repeated, if certain conditions are fulfilled. To quote Wilson himself, "There are groups-large groups-of religious believers who do use the same system of verification for religious assertions by means of their common experiences. Their experiences are not only common, but co-recurrent .... Religious assertions, then, do concern matters of public interest, at least within the religious groups who use the same verification-system for their assertions. They are publicly verifiable at least to a limited public."[23] Now, Wilson goes on to argue, if common and co-recurrent religious experiences can occur and actually do occur to persons in the religious group, there seems no bar, at least in principle, or in point of logic, why such experiences may not occur to all. The only need is that one is 'Sympathetically inclined' towards the possibility of such experiences, has a general acquaintance with religion and approaches the matter with a clear mind.[24] Wilson actually develops certain points by way of making certain conditions which if fulfilled religious experiences may occur to any one and also to the same person in a repeatable way—

    a.    The mind be freed from the direction of the senses.

    b.    The mind be trained to experience something general beneath the myriad particulars of the world.

c. A certain mental attitude, a general, unprejudiced interest in the possibility of religious experience.[25]

Now, with all our regard for the seriousness and sincerity of Wilson's attempt to put the religious statements in the same logical boat as that of the scientific or ordinary factual statements, we must point out that he does not really succeed in doing so. Firstly, we must point out that a group, even a large group, cannot mean 'public'; it cannot be equivalent to 'all'. Secondly, Wilson argues that because religious experiences occur to a large group, logically it is possible that they may occur to all. But we see that from the fact that religious experiences occur to only a group of people, the religious group, a conclusion just reverse to that of Wilson follows. That religious experiences occur to only religious people and not to all, clearly shows that they are open to only those who are bound by a common commitment, a common conviction and not to all those who do not share such convictions. This has a clear implication that religious statements do not refer to and describe an objective reality, that religious experiences do not reveal an objective fact, rather they express merely the common convictions of a particular group of people. Those who are unaware of or untouched with such convictions can in no way have religious experiences. And really speaking Wilson and all other who try a defence like him have themselves spoken of such commitment as a necessary condition for the occurrence of religious experiences. It is in this vein of laying down the conditions that Mascall speaks of 'purity of heart and religious devotion'[26], Wilson speaks of 'sympathetic inclination towards the possibility of religious experiences', B. Mitchell speaks of a 'religious tradition of the community',[27] and H.D. Lewis writes the following lines: "I do not know what it would mean at all to encounter God independently of what I believe His character and activity to be or what He requires of me in some situation."[28] How can then religious experiences claim genuine objectivity when the very precondition for their occurrence is a prior commitment? How can religious statements claim a genuine factual status like that of scientific statements under these conditions? Or, as Paul Schmidt remarks in this connection: "How can we critically and dispassionately appraise a view when the first condition for testing it is a commitment which forces us to relinquish our impartial position?" Here is a great contrast between scientific and religious statements and it is useless to attempt to put both of them in the same logical boat. Speaking of the difference between the experiences of a scientific and those of a religious man in this light, Milmed, Bella K. amply remarks, "He (scientist) is careful not to see certain results because he wants to see them... Religious experience, on the other hand is utterly unattainable unless we not only know what we are looking for but make an effort to perceive what we want to perceive."[30] Wilson, no doubt, does not simply point out the logical possibility of religious experiences occurring to all, but also, as we have seen above, formulates certain conditions, which if fulfilled, such experiences will occur to all. But the points he lays down in this connection show nothing more than the fact that for having religious experience one must first have a religious inclination, a religious attitude and that is nothing different from what we have seen and examined so far.

And above all, we must point out that the very idea of undertaking a public-test in case of the religious statements like that of scientific statements is gratuitous. Wilson himself and all those who speak with him call God a mystery. How can such a mysterious object be a subject-matter of public test? Whatever efforts one may make in the light of the conditions laid down by Wilson it is not possible to see God unless one has an inner conviction, an inner eye, to see God. Public tests, then, in the fashion of those carried out in the case of scientific statements are impossible not only due to certain practical or technical difficulties, but due to the very nature of the case. C.B. Martin very rightly remarks in this connection, "It must be made clear in conclusion that the lack of tests and checking procedures which has been noted is not merely an unfortunate result of human frailty. It is necessarily the nature of the case."[31] Further, if religious statements are to be tested like scientific statements, they become mere provisional hypotheses to be accepted or rejected on such tests. But where do the religious believers treat religious statements as hypotheses? They rather assert these statements with a sense of total commitment. And hence any talk of public test in case of religious statements seems going against the real nature of such statements. The firmness with which such statements are asserted and observed clearly shows that they are more appropriate as expressing the inner conviction of the believers than as describing a fact.

Furthermore, even if it is granted for the time-being that verification with reference to the experience of a group of people logically implies the possibility of public verification of religious statements and that there is even a propriety, for such a test, where are such tests still similar to those carried in the case of scientific statements? The sense-experiences that many have in relation to a particular object or event or situation are more or less the same or similar, as is known from the detailed descriptions that all of them give of such experiences, but religious experiences differ, sometimes sharply. If religious experiences are the experiences of a common objective situation, then such experiences must tally in details. Wilson actually claims that such experiences are not only common but co-recurrent. facts do not testify to the truth of Wilson's contention. He says that within the religious group, religious experiences are not only common but co-recurrent. But does religious group mean only the Christian group? The religious experience that the Hindu group has sharply differs from one that occurs to a Christian or a Muslim. The descriptions contained in world-religions which are all allegedly based upon certain religious experiences of their prophets and saints hardly coincide. And even in case of persons belonging to the same religious group, sometimes such experiences are not similar. Even within the Hindu group, a worshipper of Rama has an experience of Rama, a worshipper of Siva has that of Siva and so on, although it is granted in principle that all these different gods are the different forms of the same God. The above considerations clearly show that religious experiences are not common, co-recurrent and similar even amongst the persons of the religious group itself. Such experiences are all based on individual, social or traditional pre-possessions. Or again, we may say that they seem to be the results of not a dispassionate scientific enquiry, but of a personal or social conviction. How can then religious statements claim the same verifiable status as that of the scientific statements? Where are religious statements verified with reference to common or similar experiences of different persons just in the same way in which scientific statements are verified with reference to common and co-recurrent sense-experiences?

The above considerations clearly demonstrate that religious statements cannot legitimately claim a factual status similar to that of scientific statements. They are not only not scientific statements, but are also not *like* scientific statements. However, certain attempts are still made to retain the genuinely factual or cognitive status of religious statements on some shirking grounds. Here a point-to-point comparison of religious experience with the sense-experience is not attempted, rather it is accepted whole heartedly that due to the unique and mysterious nature of the object of religious experience, such an experience cannot literally bear a comparison with sense-experience and hence the question of public test or check does not seem at all relevant in the former case. But still, it is insisted, religious experiences are perfectly objective and therefore the religious statements are factual in the genuine sense of the term. Such a plea is advanced by way of making a distinction between two kinds of relationships, originally brought about, perhaps, by Martin Buber. It is held that the relationship of a person to a sense-object is one in which only one side is lively and responding, whereas the relationship (or experience) in which God is revealed to man is an 'I-Thou' relationship, a person-to-person encounter in which both the sides are lively and responding. Thus, the religious relationship cannot bear a direct comparison with the sense-object relationship. But still the religious relationship is a genuine subject-object relationship and the 'Thou' represents a perfectly objective situation. But to such a plea one may reply that even if religious experience is taken as a case of person-to-person encounter as contrasted with person-to-object relationship, where is the basic issue altered? The question of a public verification remains to be solved even if the objective situation is that of a lively, responding 'Thou'. As Hepburn very rightly asks in this context, "Are there no checking-procedures relevant to the encounter of person with person? Or does all 'checking' necessarily degrade persons to status of things? If the vital analogy here is that between meeting people and meeting God, have the theologians established this analogy firmly enough to bear the weighty superstructure that they have erected upon it?"[32] However, if by the uniqueness of the 'I-Thou' relationship, it is intended to be maintained that such a relationship (or experience) is not possible to an unconcerned, neutral observer in the same coercive way as the experience of a material object (It) is possible, that such an experience requires what the existentialists like Buber and Tillich would call a sense of personal 'involvement' into or 'participation' with the object of experience (the "Thou), then we are certainly not to dispute the uniqueness. But then on this sense of uniqueness, the genuine objectivity of religious experiences cannot be maintained. If the experience of Thou requires a personal involvement on the part of the observer, if the experience is not possible, without a personal commitment, if the 'Thou' is not to be revealed to a disinterested neutral observer, then where does the 'Thou' remain genuinely objective? It is only *relatively* objective, i.e., objective for an interested, committed I. And thus, where do the religious statements remain genuinely factual and cognitive? They become the statements expressing a personal conviction, a personal commitment. Of course, corresponding to his conviction, the man sometimes has certain revelations before him in which he seems to face an objective situation, but the situation has. only an *objective force* for him, it is not *genuinely objective*.

A still another plea to maintain the factuality of religious statements is made by way of maintaining that because the object to which such statements refer is unique, mysterious and infinite, it is not possible to have a clear and exhaustive picture of him in religious experiences. Therefore, religious statements are metaphorical, parabolic and analogical. Their meanings are not literally clear and therefore ordinary public tests may not be carried out in case of them. Moreover, because the infinite reality is not exhaustively apprehended by each one in all its aspects, therefore, differences in reports may be there and hence all may not undergo the same verification-procedure for the statements. But still from this it does not follow that religious statements do not say anything about a reality. They say, as Wilson suggests, at least something about the reality. To such pleas, we will answer that if God is infinite and mysterious and his infinite and mysterious character is never fully revealed to anyone, how is one even entitled to say that he is infinite and mysterious? How does one know that he is infinitely powerful (omnipotent), infinitely knowing (omniscient) etc.? It is said that such phrases are metaphorically or parabolically meaningful in case of God, but we will see just now in a succeeding section that such appeals made to metaphorical or parabolic or analogical predication in order to save the factual and descriptive nature of religious statements also do not succeed in their attempts. What we are made to conclude thus on the basis of a consideration of the verifiability of religious statements with reference to religious experience is that religious statements can't be taken factual and cognitive in the same sense in which ordinary factual or scientific statements are taken. A critical examination of the appeal made to religious experience for the verification of religious statements itself shows that such experiences are possible to only those who have a prior inner faith in God. And hence religious statements may have a factual or objective status for only those who are within the circle of religious faith and never for all. In other words, religious statements may have only, what we may call, a 'convictional' or 'relative' factuality, but they cannot be taken as having factuality as hard and genuine as that of ordinary factual or scientific statements.

## REFERENCES

1. F. R. Tennant, *'Philosophical Theology'*, Vol. II (Cambridge University Press, 1928-30).
2. From a selection entitled 'Is Theological Discourse Possible?' taken from K.L. Mascall's bock

'Words and Images' and included in *Philosophy of Religion* (New York, Macmillan, 1962), edited by Abernethy and Langgord, p. 251.

3. To this end Lewis devotes his entire book *'Our Experience of God'* (George Allen & Unwin, London, 1959) and his essays Recent Empiricism and Religion', *Philosophy*, July, 1957 and The Cognitive Factor in Religious Experience, Proceedings of the Aristotelian Society, Suppl. Vol. XXIX.

4. H.D. Lewis, *Our Experience of God*, p. 23.

5. Ibid., Chapter II. Also, an essay God and Mystery' by H.D. Lewis, included in *Prospects for Metaphysics'* (New York, Philosophical Library, 1961), edited by Ian T. Ramsey.

6. H.D. Lewis, *Ibid.*, p. 47.

7. John Wilson, *Language & Christian Belief* (London, Macmillan & Co., 1958), p. 5.

8. *Ibid.*, p. 11.

9. *Ibid.*, p. 16.

10. John Wilson, *Philosophy and Religion* London, Oxford University Press, 1961), pp. 61-62.

11. *Ibid.*, p. 71.

12. *Language and Christian Belief*, p. 13.

13. *Ibid.*, p. 14.

14. *Ibid.*, p. 11.

15. A.C. Ewing 'Awareness of God', *Philosophy*, Vol. XL, No. 151, January, 1965.

16. *Ibid.*, p.1.

17. *Ibid.*, p. 4.

18. *Ibid.*, p. 8.

19. Included in *'Faith and Logic'* (George Allen & Uwin, 1957), ed. by Basil Mitchell.

20. Ian. T. Ramsey, *'Religious Language'* (S.C.M. London, 1957).
21. *Language & Christian Belief*, p. 20.
22. *Ibid.,* p 21.
23. *Ibid.,* pp. 24-25.
24. *Ibid.,* p. 26f.
25. *Philosophy and Religion*, p. 91.
26. E.L. Mascall, *op. cit.*, in Abernethy & Langford's *Philosophy of Religion*, p. 251.
27. B. Mitchell, 'The Grace of God' in *'Faith & Logic'*, edited by B. Mitchell, p. 161.
28. H.D. Lewis, *'Our Experience of God'*, p. 47.
29. Paul. F. Schmidt, *Religious Knowledge* (Free Press of Glancoe, 1961), p. 55.
30. Milmed, Bella K., 'Theories of Religious Knowledge from Kant to Jaspers', *Philosophy*. Vol. 29, 1954, p. 207. (However, we do not approve of the use of the verb 'wants' here which has a Freudian note about it and which tends to make religious experiences something purely subjective and a matter of wishful thinking. We approve of Milmed's spirit so far as in a general way it tries to bring about a distinction between the experience of a scientist and that of a religious believer on the ground that while the experience of the former does not require any prior commitment, the experience in the latter case necessarily does so.)
31. C.B. Martin, 'A Religious Way of Knowledge' in *New Essays in Philosophical Theology*, p. 95.
32. 32.R.W. Hepburn, *'Christianity and Paradox'* (C.A. Watts & Co. London, 1958), p. 30.

## Section II
## PROOFS FOR THE EXISTENCE OF GOD

In general, the question of the factuality of religious belief (or statements) is a question of the existence of God and the two can't be separated. God, in general, is the subject of all religious statements and for those who want to maintain the factual status of religious statements, i.e., who want to maintain that these statements refer to some objective fact, must have to show that the subject-term 'God' is applicable to a real objective fact. This has more often been attempted by trying to prove the reality of God on logical grounds by means of certain arguments. Such proofs for the existence of God have been advanced from very old days and consequently they have got a history. At one time someone advanced a particular proof, at another time some other thinker attacked the validity of that proof and advanced his own different sort of proof instead. For example, Thomas Aquinas criticised the proof of Anselm, but in his turn advanced the so-called important 'five ways' of proving God. But here instead of going into the troublesome detailed history, we shall take up for our known by the famous well-known traditional proofs popularly known by the famous names of Ontological proof, Cosmological proof, Causal proof etc.

The proofs or arguments for the existence of God may be broadly divided into *a priori* and *a posteriori*. An *a priori* proof starts from the very concept of the Supreme Being as its basis and proves therefrom his existence: An *a posteriori* proof proceeds not from the concept of God but from the facts of common experience as its basis and sees through them a necessary reference to the Divine Being. Of the four traditional proofs—the Ontological, the Causal, the Cosmological and the Teleological—only the first one is taken as an *a priori* proof; the latter three are included under the second category. We shall consider all these proofs one by one here. Besides, we shall consider one more proof, the Moral one, which in one of its forms cannot at all be regarded as a rational proof, while in its another form it may be regarded as a kind of a posteriori proof.

## i. The Proofs

### (a) The Ontological Proof

Of the various proofs for the existence of the Supreme Being the ontological proof has drawn the attention of the thinkers— both ancient and modern-the most. It is generally believed to have been first propounded by St. Anselm in his *Proslogian*. Later on, the argument was developed by Descartes and Leibnitz in their own ways. We shall, however, present the argument here mainly on the basis of St. Anselm's *Proslogian* and Descartes' *Meditations*.

The central point of the argument seems to be that, the existence of the Supreme Being is implied in the very concept of such a being. In other words, the existence of God follows necessarily from the very concept of God. What, after all, is this concept of God? According to St. Anselm, the concept of God. is the concept of "something than which nothing greater can be conceived". Now, if God is conceived as non-existing, the concept of God will not be the concept of something than which a greater cannot be conceived. For, to conceive God as non-existing means that God is in the conception alone, and not in reality. But to be in conception and reality both is definitely greater than to be in the conception alone. And, therefore, if God be in the conception alone, the concept of God will not be the concept of something than which greater nothing can be conceived. In consequence, the concept of something than which a greater cannot be conceived will be the concept of something than which a greater can be conceived. And this is a plain contradiction. Therefore, something than which nothing greater can be conceived must be in reality too, besides being in conception. And this means that God exists. To quote Anselm's own words in this connection, "And certainly that than which a greater cannot be conceived—cannot stand only in relation to the understanding. For if it stands at least in relation to the understanding, it can be conceived to be also reality, and this is something greater. Therefore, if 'that than which a greater cannot be conceived' only stood in relation to the understanding, then 'that than which a greater cannot be conceived' would be something than which a greater can be conceived. But this is certainly impossible. Therefore, something than which a greater cannot be conceived undoubtedly both stands in relation to the understanding and exists in reality."[1]

As a matter of fact, Anselm through his famous ontological argument proves not only the existence of God, but also his *necessary* existence. For this purpose, he employs a separate related argument in his *Proslogian*, Chapter III. Although this has been always recognised that Anselm proved not only the existence of God but also his necessary existence through his argument, but it is perhaps Norman Malcolm, a reputed Wittgensteinian, who first of all draws our attention to the presence of two arguments, instead of one, in Anselm's proof for the existence of God.[2] According to him, the first argument given in *Proslogian*, Chapter II, proves the existence of God and the second given in *Proslogian*, Chapter III, proves his necessary existence. Here again in his second argument, Anselm, as in his first one, uses a *Reductio ad absurdum* to prove that God's existence is necessary, that "something than which a greater cannot be conceived so truly is that it is impossible even to conceive of it as not existing." He argues that if something than which a greater cannot be conceived be such that its non-existence can be conceived, then that the non-existence of which cannot be conceived will definitely be greater. And in that case, there will again arise a contradiction. As Anselm himself says, "If that than which a greater cannot be conceived could be conceived not to be, we would have an impossible contradiction: that than which a greater cannot be conceived would not be that than which a greater cannot be conceived."[3] This shows that the non-existence of God is impossible, that he exists necessarily.

Essentially the same argument is later on developed by Descartes in his *Meditations*. Descartes defines God as "a supremely perfect being" and argues that existence is as necessary and inseparable a characteristic of God as the three angles being equal to have right angles is the essential and inseparable characteristic of a triangle. To be a supremely perfect being, God has not to lack in anything. He can, therefore, not lack in existence also. Existence is an inseparable property of God. As Descartes himself says, "Existence can no more be separated from the essence (of definition) of God than can its having three angles equal to two right angles be separated from the essence of a (rectilinear) triangle or the idea of a mountain from the idea of valley; and so there is not any less repugnance to our conceiving of God (that is, a Being supremely perfect) to whom existence is lacking (that is to say, to whom a certain perfection is lacking), then to conceive of a mountain which has no valley."[4]

From the above, it is clear that Descartes' argument is not really different from that of Anselm; only the former makes existence more explicitly a predicate or attribute of God which he cannot lack, if he has to be the supremely perfect being. This point is involved in Anselm's argument also, only Descartes makes it more explicit. According to both of them, existence is a perfection Which the most perfect being or the being greater than whom nothing can be conceived cannot lack. It is really this point which has proved in the history of the ontological argument to be the most fascinating for those who have tried to reflect on the argument. Kant brought the point in the forefront in course of his criticism of the Cartesian argument and since then it has become the focal point of discussion amongst thinkers. We shall see the criticism of the ontological argument based on this point below, but before going to that we shall see certain other criticisms.

The ontological argument has been criticised since its very inception into philosophy. Gaunilon, a contemporary of Anselm, seems to be its first critic. Gaunilon points out that the logic of the ontological argument, if strictly adhered to, leads to very absurd conclusions. Basing on the logic of the ontological argument, Gaunilon says, one can prove the existence of not only the most perfect being, God, but also of, say, the most perfect island. If one has the idea of the most perfect island as one more perfect than which nothing can be conceived, then the island must exist also, because without existence it will lack perfection, and that island which is in idea and existence both will be more perfect than it. Gaunilon really seems emphasizing the point that it is simply absurd to claim proving the real existence of anything from the mere idea or conception of that thing. There is a big gap between abstract idea and concrete existence.

Anselm tried to save his argument against Gaunilon's criticism by taking shelter in the uniqueness of God-concept which involved not only existence, but *necessary* existence. The concept of nothing else involved this *necessary* existence and therefore the existence of nothing else could be proved on the line of the ontological proof for the existence of God. This plea, we may see, may with some plausibility withstand criticism against the second of Anselm's ontological proofs, but how far can it withstand Gaunilon's criticism against the first of the arguments is a matter of grave doubt. We shall, however, not be very much preoccupied here with Gaunilon's criticism of Anselm's argument or arguments. The most important phase of the discussions and debate about the ontological argument comes with Immanuel Kant's criticisms which he develops in the Transcendental Dialectic of his *Critique of Pure Reason*. Kant's criticisms are really directed against the Cartesian version of the ontological proof, but we have seen that there is no substantial difference between Anselm's and Descartes' versions of the same.

Kant first of all directs his attention to the Cartesian claim that the idea of existence belongs as necessarily and inseparably to the concept of God as the idea of having three angles (or the three angles being together equal to two right angles) belongs necessarily and inseparably to the concept of a triangle. Kant points out that such a plea in no way proves either the real existence of a triangle with its three angles or of God. What it. shows is that in each case the predicate is analytically related with the subject, but that does not become able to show that the subject along with its predicate actually exists. If the subject is. accepted, the predicate has to be accepted, because the two are analytically related, but there is no harm rejecting both the subject and the predicate together. As Kant says, "To posit a triangle and yet to reject its three angles, is self-contradictory: but there is no self-contradiction in rejecting the triangle-together with its three angles. The same holds true of the concept of an absolutely necessary being."[5]

Kant's main point of criticism against the ontological argument, however, centres around the question whether existence is a predicate. We have seen that at least the Cartesian version of the ontological argument explicitly regards existence as an attribute or predicate of God, lacking in which he will be less perfect. Kant's point seems to be that although existence or 'exists' may be regarded as a grammatical predicate, it cannot be taken as a real predicate. A real predicate is that which adds something to the idea or concept of the thing to which it is applied. For example, when we say about something that it is red or round we add something to the concept of that thing. such that with any one of the above properties the thing will be something other than what it would be without any or all of them. In other words, such predicates if added to the idea of something add to its content. But existence is not such a predicate. When we say of something that it exists, we add nothing to its content. We simply say that it is, which is no addition to its original contents. As Kant very aptly says in this connection, "*Being* is evidently not a real predicate, that is, a conception of something which is added to the conception of some other thing. It is merely the positing of a thing... logically, it is merely the copula of a judgment .... Thus, the real contains no more than the possible. A hundred real dollars contain no more than a hundred possible dollars. The contents of both are exactly the same. Only the latter indicates the conception and the former the object."[6] Thus when we say of anything that it exists, we do not add anything to its content, rather we apply the concept of the thing to the actual world. When after describing many qualities of a man, one also adds that he exists, he really adds nothing to the qualities of the man. Moore tries to establish the above Kantian point in his own way by contrasting 'exists' with 'growls'.[7] He uses the two predicates in relation to the subject Some tame tigers' and points out that while the negative of 'Some tame tigers growl' (i.e., 'some tame tigers do not growl') has a perfectly clear sense, the negative of 'Some tame tigers exist' (i.e., 'Some tame tigers do not exist) does not make any sense. By this example, Moore actually wants to illustrate that while 'growls' is a genuine predicate which adds something to the content or character of something, 'exists' is no such predicate. Had 'exists' been a genuine predicate like 'growls', then both the affirmative and negative uses of the former would have made sense like those of the latter. But while the affirmative use of the former in relation to 'some tame tigers' makes sense it does not make sense in its negative use with the same subject-term. This shows that 'exists' is not a genuine predicate like other such predicates as 'growls', 'loves' etc.

The point regarding the question, whether existence is a predicate has claimed such a vast portion of contemporary philosophical discussions that it is really hard to count on fingers how many recent philosophers have reflected upon the problem.[8] Almost all them have argued that existence can't be taken as a real predicate. After Kant, it is perhaps Russell who re-initiated the discussion in contemporary philosophy in the year 1919. Russell set forth the view that existence could not be the predicate of individuals; it was rather a property of propositional functions or classes or concepts. According to Russell, whenever we say about an individual object that it exists, it makes absolutely no sense. It makes sense only in relation to a class or concept. For example, when we say that 'Tables exist', it means 'There are x's such that x is a table is true'. In other words, it simply means that the concept of table is applicable to at least one real object in the world. It does not mean in any case that the attribute of existence is being given to tables. It is difficult to bring forth the detailed merits of these observations here, but this much seems clear by all these that existence cannot be regarded as an attribute of something. If so, it does not seem correct to say that the idea of existence, if added to the idea of God, will make it more perfect and, if subtracted from it, will make it less perfect. The logic of the ontological argument is definitely based upon such a view and therefore it is logically mistaken. It is not able to prove the real existence of God by taking existence as an inseparable character of the idea of God.

Although for some time the point that existence is not a predicate was taken as crucial to the refutation of the ontological proof, afterwards it was realised by certain thinkers that it was not as crucial as it was taken to be and there were other more important considerations involved in the argument itself which would make it thoroughly unworthy of its purpose. For example, J. Shaffer in his important essay, 'Existence, Predication and the Ontological Argument' tries to show that in the way in which Kant and others try to prove that existence is not a predicate, even 'red' cannot be a predicate.[10] In fact, according to him, in that manner nothing can be a predicate. As he says, "The argument which shows that 'exists' is not a 'real' predicate also shows that nothing could be one." Shaffer wants to emphasize another point which seems to him to be more crucial for proving the worthlessness of the ontological argument. Similarly, George Nakhnikian and Wesley C. Salmon try to show in an article entitled '"Exists" as a predicate', that even if it is conceded that existence is a predicate, it does nothing to help ontological argument prove the real existence of God.[11] For, what, after all, will the ontological argument gain by having existence as a predicate? Perhaps it will be able thereby to get its point supported that existence will be included within the defining characteristic of God. This is what the ontological argument really wants to do when it says that existence is included within the very concept of God, that it is a necessary character of God such that in the absence of it, God will no longer remain God. But does the argument become able to prove the real existence of God in this manner? Certainly not. What it becomes able to establish is simply that, existence forms a necessary part of the concept of God, that existence is analytically contained in the idea of God, that 'God' is to be defined in terms of 'existence' or rather necessary 'existence'. But defining something in terms of existence or even in terms of necessary existence does not make it really existent. Anselm and Descartes seem to emphasize through the ontological argument that God must exist, because "God does not exist' is a self-contradiction. But they fail to see that by taking 'God does not exist' as a self-contradiction, they simply become able to show that 'God exists' is a tautology, which in its turn shows that 'exists' is the meaning of the term 'God' and not that there really is a God.

The point is very ably clarified by J. Shaffer in his essay referred to above. There he points out that the entire strength of the ontological argument lies in an illegitimate move from an intentional to an extensional use of the term 'God' in the sentence 'God exists'. The argument starts with the assertion that 'existence' is a logical requirement of the concept of God, because for want of it the concept will not be the concept of the most perfect being. So far it simply defines 'God' in terms of 'existence' and thus uses the term 'God' only intentionally in the sentence God exists. But on the basis of this intentional use of the term 'God', it makes an unwarranted leap to its extensional use when it takes the sentence 'God exists' to mean that there really is a God. Here in the second case, it uses the term 'God' in the sense of its applicability to a real object. Thus, according to Shaffer, the argument "conceals the illicit move from an intentional to an extensional statement."[12] 'God exists' and 'There is a God' are not identical statements according to Shaffer. The former is a tautology, the latter is an existential statement. And yet, the ontological argument makes an illicit move from the former to the latter. To put the point more effectively and beautifully, Shaffer compares concepts to nets.[13] He says that one can make a net of any size and may validly claim that the net catches a fish of that size. But whether there is really a fish of that size to which the net may be applied is a different question altogether. The existence of the fish of a particular size is not proved by the presence of a net of that size. Similarly, one may analyse the concept of God in any way he likes, say, as necessarily existing, but whether the concept applies to any actually existing being is a different question altogether. The real existence of God is not proved by defining 'God' as necessarily existing. Basically, the same point was being emphasized by Kant also when he remarked, "the real object. the dollars-is not analytically contained in my conception but forms a synthetical addition to my conception....."[14]

We have thus seen that the attempts made by Anselm and Descartes to prove the existence of God on purely *a priori* grounds have been thoroughly refuted by thinkers, both ancient and modern. But our account of the refutation will not be complete unless we mention here one ingenious attempt made by J.N. Findlay[15] to erect an ontological disproof of the existence of God on the lines of Anselm's ontological proof. The nerve of Anselm's proof, we have seen, consists in the point that, the existence of God follows necessarily from the very concept of God. As opposed to it, Findlay tries to show that not Gods existence, but his necessary non-existence or the impossibility of his existence follow inevitably from the very concept of God. Taking clue from Anselm himself the concept of God is the concept of something that which nothing greater can be conceived, Findlay argue that God to be God must exist necessarily and possess all his attributes in a necessary manner. But the trouble, according to Findlay, is that such a being could not exist, that the existence of such a being is an impossibility. As Findlay himself says, "It was indeed an ill day for Anselm when he hit upon his famous proof. For on that day, he not only laid bare something that is of the essence of an adequate religious object, but also something that entails its necessary non-existence."[16] Findlay constructs his ontological disproof on what he calls the 'modern' view of the "necessity in pro-positions". Modern view seems to restrict the use of the adjectives 'necessary' and 'contingent' only to propositions. Objects, therefore, are not to be characterised as necessary and contingent. On this view, the statement that God is a necessary being or that the existence of God is necessary is to be translated as " 'God exists' is a necessary proposition". And on a still another modern view according to Findlay, holding this is 'self-evidently absurd', because no existential proposition could be necessary; only tautologies could be so. To quote Findlay himself, "And, on a yet modern view of the matter, necessity in propositions merely reflects our use of words, the arbitrary conventions of our language."[17] Thus, if the proposition 'God exists' is necessary, it simply reflects the arbitrary convention of our use of certain words and therefore does not refer to any real existential situation. If it, however, claims to be genuinely existential, it cannot be necessary because existentially necessary propositions are impossible. Thus, God's existence is either contingent nor impossible. The former is not worthy of the conception of God and hence meaningless, the latter shows the impossibility of God's existence. As Findlay himself concludes that the very requirements of God-concept plainly "entail not only that there isn't a God, but that the Divine Existence is either senseless or impossible."[18]

The above ontological disproof of Findlay has been mainly criticised on two grounds—(1) That there can be no existentially necessary propositions, may be true with regard to our ordinary statements, but it is not necessary that the principle will equally apply to statements about God: these statements may be existential and necessary both at the same time (Hughes[19] and Malcolm[20]). (2) Necessity of God's existence is not the same as the necessity of propositions about God. Findlay's entire disproof is based on his confusion between the two (Rainer[21] and Hutchings[22]). But such criticisms may be easily disposed off. Hughes asserts that propositions about God may be both existential and necessary, but he does not explain how they can be so. Malcolm's plea that there are religious systems in which God figures as a necessary belief is no proof of the point that statements about God are existential and necessary.

Many illogical and absurd things may be present in religious systems, but their presence in those systems does not prove that they are right or rational. May be that it is on the basis of the uniqueness of God-concept or God-statements that statements about God are regarded as both existential and necessary. But that is really taking shelter in faith and mysticism by leaving aside the canons of logic. As Allen very rightly remarks in this connection, "To proffer the uniqueness of the concept of God as an intuitive ground for the ontological argument is to abandon rules of logic for the eye of faith. The faith may be well founded: the argument is bad."[23] What Findlay wants to show is not that the existence of a necessary being cannot be maintained on any ground, but that on principles of rational thinking, we cannot do so. Rainer and Hutchings point out that Findlay has confused between necessity of God's existence and the necessity of the propositions about him, but Findlay is actually concerned with the latter, i.e., with our thinking about the necessity of God which is expressed through propositions about him. Findlay clearly accepts that his disproof has got no value for those who "might come to perceive the necessity of God's existence in some higher mystical state"[24] or for those who think that religion is a unique sphere where the principles of ordinary logic are not applicable.

Hence, we think Findlay has succeeded in showing that on valid principles of logical thinking, one cannot maintain the necessary existence of God. And thus, either the logical absurdity of the notion of God or else the absurdity of his existence.

After the criticisms of Kant, it was more or less taken as granted by the thinkers that the ontological argument now had no strength to stand. The recent criticisms of the analytic thinkers all the more added to this conviction. But strangely and unexpectedly enough, recent philosophy has seen two very important defences of the argument-one at the hands of an eminent Wittgensteinian, Norman Malcolm,[25] and another at those of Charles Hartshorne.[26] Although the defence of the latter is a bit formalised in the symbolism of modal logic, still the defences of both the thinkers proceed essentially on the same line. Both have actually defended what has been taken as the second ontological argument of Anselm. Both the thinkers seem inclined to hold that although existence is not a predicate of God, necessary existence is one, and therefore although the first Anselmian argument is invalid, the second one is valid.

The second actually proves that God's existence is necessary or that God exists necessarily and this in turn implies that God exists. Hence, through his second argument Anselm becomes able to prove the existence of God.

Analysing the second ontological argument which makes for its chief basis the assertion that necessary existence is the predicate of God, Malcolm and Hartshorne point out that what Anselm wants to convey through his argument is that Perfection (or God) cannot exist contingently, that it must either not exist at all or exist necessarily. As Hartshorne remarks in this connection, "It is to be noted that Anselm's Principle does not say that perfection would be imperfect if it were unexemplified, but that anything exemplifying it merely contingently would be imperfect, and would not exemplify it after all."[27] Similarly Malcolm remarks, "What Anselm has proved is that the notion of contingent existence or of contingent non-existence cannot have any application to God. His existence must either be logically necessary or logically impossible."[28] Then after this they say on behalf of Anselm that God's existence will be impossible only if the concept of God is self-contradictory. Assuming that it is not so, because the concept of God according to Anselm is the concept of something than which nothing greater can be conceived and apparently there is no contradiction in this concept, it follows that God's existence is logically necessary. Malcolm summarises the relevant portion of the Anselmian proof in this connection as follows, "If God, a being a greater than which cannot be conceived, does not exist, then he cannot *come* into existence. For if he did, he would either have been *caused* to come into existence or have *happened* to come into existence, and in either case he would be a limited being, which by our conception of him he is not. Since he cannot come into existence, if he does not exist, his existence is impossible. If he does exist, he cannot have come into existence (for the reasons given), nor can he cease to exist, for nothing could cause him to cease to exist nor could it just happen that he ceased to exist. So if God exists, his existence is necessary. Thus,

God's existence is either impossible or necessary. It can be the former only if the concept of such a being is self-contradictory or in some way logically absurd. Assuming that this is not so, it follows that he necessarily exists."[29]

This argument attributed originally to St. Anselm reveals one point of special modal importance in case of the existence of God. If God is conceivable, his existence is not impossible. That is, if God is conceivable, his existence is possible. And the very possibility of his existence ensures or rather implies his necessary existence. For we have seen that his existence is cither impossible or necessary and now if it is assumed that it is not impossible (i.e., possible), it follows that it is necessary (p v q; p, q). Thus, in case of God, the very possibility of his existence implies his necessary existence. It is perhaps to this aspect of the ontological argument that Leibnitz drew our attention. Recently Hartshorne has taken this modal aspect of the argument for his consideration. Hartshorne has actually drawn the modal structure of the second Anselmian argument by starting from the premise that, in case of God (Perfection), the very possibility of his existence implies his necessary existence i.e., if Perfection exists, it exists necessarily. Hartshorne's modal structure of the argument is as follows:[30]

1. q → Nq — "Anselm's Principle": perfection could not exist contingently (hence, the assertion that it exists could not be contingently but only necessarily true).
2. Nq V ~Nq — Excluded Middle.
3. ~Nq → N~Nq — Form of Becker's postulate: Modal status is always necessary.
4. Nq V N ~Nq — Inference from (2, 3).
5. N~Nq → N~q — Inference from (1): the

necessary falsity of the Consequent implies that of the antecedent (Modal form of modus tollens).

6. Nq V N~q — Inference from (4,5).
7. ~N ~q — Intuitive postulate: Perfection is not impossible.
8. Nq. — Inference from (6,7).
9. Nq → q. — Modal axiom.
10. q — Inference from (8,9).

(In this argument, 'q' stands for (∃x) Px', i.e., 'there is a perfect being, or perfection exists'. 'N' stands for 'It is necessary (logically true) that; '~ stands for 'It is not true that'; V stands for 'or'; '→ stands for 'strictly implies', such that 'p → q' is equivalent to 'N~(p & ~q). Thus, the above structure tries to show that second ontological argument proves the existence of God through a valid logical process of modal logic.

Now let us see to some extent the question of the validity of the arguments which Malcolm and Hartshorne have erected on behalf of Anselm. Let us take up Hartshorne's first. As a matter of fact, the very first proposition in Hartshorne's proof seems very much dubious. The first proposition says that the truth of a proposition (q) strictly implies the logically necessary truth of that proposition (Nq). This simply means that if a proposition is true, it is true by logical necessity. But it is quite obvious that no valid logical principle would allow such an implication. Specially, when 'q' is an existential proposition, it cannot be logically necessary. If it is taken as logically necessary, then in Perfection exists' (a), the term 'Perfection (God) is being used only intentionally and exists' is just its logical meaning. From this intentional statement as the basis, then, when finally 'g' or 'God exists' is proved, that also must be only an intentional statement and not an extensional one, as the argument certainly wishes it to be. In the middle course of the argument also, there is no proposition which may logically warrant a transition from the original intentional statement to an extensional one. Perhaps Hartshorne's insistence here would be that in the unique case of God, existential proposition may be necessary and Anselm actually intended that to be when he said, perfection could not exist contingently. But this is again forsaking the grounds of logic in favour of faith and mysticism. No logic prohibits us from conceiving the non-existence of a being whose existence we can conceive. Hume was quite right when he said, "whatever we conceive as existent, we can also conceive as non-existent. There is no being therefore whose non-existence implies a contraction."[31] If at all we want to maintain the necessary existence of God, we can do so, as Hick rightly points out, in the sense of *ontological* necessity, and not in the sense of logical necessity.[32] According to Hick, as a matter of fact, when Anselm also took God as a necessary being, he took him to be so only in the sense of an ontologically necessary being, and not in the sense of a logically necessary being. Scriptures also, according to Hick, take God as necessary in the sense of ontological necessity. Hick points out, and perhaps rightly, that a being can only be ontologically necessary. What can be logically necessary is a proposition. So we must distinguish between the ontological necessity of a being and the logical necessity of a proposition. A being is called ontologically necessary according to him when it is taken as existing without beginning or end and without dependence upon anything other than itself. A proposition is logically necessary when it is true by definition." Taking the existence of God of Perfection as ontologically necessary, we can very well maintain the modal relation 'q-Nq' and proceed validly up to proposition no. 6 in Hartshorne's argument. But unless this proposition is established in terms of logical necessity, Hartshorne's purpose will not be served. For, unless the disjunction is established in terms of *logical* necessity and *logical* impossibility, the existence of God cannot be validly derived from it. So, henceforth, either he will have to take an illicit move from ontological to logical necessity or he will have to start from the very beginning with the notion of logical necessity as applied to the existence of God. He adopts the first course, but in this case he starts with a dubious premise which has got no valid logical backing. Hence the modal structure of the ontological argument as erected by Hartshorne does not seem proving worthy of its purpose.

Let us now come to Malcolm's argument. Malcolm's argument is clearly vitiated by a shift by him in the midcourse of his argument from the notion of ontological necessity to logical necessity in relation to the existence of God. John Hick charges both Hartshorne and Malcolm of this shift in course of their arguments when he remarks against both of them, "Two importantly different concepts of necessary being are involved in Malcolm-Hartshorne proof, and that the proof is vitiated by a shift in midcourse from one of these concepts to the other." We think that this charge is strictly validly applicable to Malcolm alone, and not to Hartshorne because the latter from the very beginning understands by 'Necessity' logical necessity.

It is a different matter that by understanding necessity in terms of logical necessity, Hartshorne has vitiated his proof from the very start. Now, in case of Malcolm,[35] it is quite clear from his analysis of the concept of God as a necessary being that he is using the term 'necessary' in the sense of ontologically necessary. But abruptly while concluding towards the end of his argument that God's existence is either impossible or necessary, he takes the words 'impossible' and 'necessary' in the sense of *logically* impossible and *logically* necessary. This is certainly an illegitimate and unwarranted shift and the whole argument is vitiated due to this.

Apart from any such specific criticisms that we have made above against the reconstructed arguments of Malcolm and Hartshorne, we will like in the end to emphasize once again the same basic point against the ontological argument and any attempted defence thereof which was formerly emphasized by Gaunilon and Kant and more recently in a very beautiful manner by J. Shaffer. The point is, whether it is, to use Findlay's words, "possible to build bridges between mere abstractions and concrete existence."[36] Understood and analysed in any ingenious fashion, the ontological argument at most becomes. able to define 'God' in terms of necessary existence' and not to prove God's necessary existence in reality. The question is, whether by simply defining 'God' in terms of necessary existence, one proves God's real existence. Even if one says that existing in reality is a necessary condition of the concept of God, then also what is proved is not the real existence of God but simply the fact that existing in reality is the defining characteristic of God such that 'God exists' is an analytic proposition. And this in the real sense is no proof for the actual existence of God.

## (b) The Causal Proof

This proof, unlike the ontological one, is an a posteriori proof which starts from an empirical premise. It constitutes the second of St. Aquinas' famous Five Ways of proving God and is also known as the Argument from the First cause of the First cause Argument. It starts from the chain of causation present in the world and argues on the basis of that for the reality of a first cause in which the chain finally ends (or, looked at from the opposite side, in which the chain originates). We find that anything we take in the world has a cause, and this cause in its turn again has a cause and so on. Now, this chain, according to Aquinas, cannot go on endlessly, because that way we shall fall in an infinite regress. The chain therefore must end somewhere (or, seen from the opposite side, must begin somewhere). In other words, there must be a first cause, the original cause of the entire chain, and this first cause is called God. The first cause is self-caused and requires no other cause for itself. It is the uncaused cause of the entire chain of events and things. Every other cause in the chain is a cause of one particular thing or event that immediately follows it, but this first cause is the cause of the entire universe, the Universe as a whole.

This first cause argument also has been criticised by philosophers from the very old days, but the recent criticisms of the argument made by the scientifically oriented thinkers are of greater logical interest. The very first criticism that is put forward against the argument is that it proves only a first cause, and not a God. The first cause to be God must be all-powerful, all-perfect, all-knowing, creator etc., which the argument does not prove. Therefore, even if it is accepted that there should be a first cause to explain the chain of causation in the world, it is not necessary that the first cause is God.

But more serious criticisms still await the argument. It is pointed out by the recent analytic thinkers that the very notion of a first cause is misleading and senseless. The hypothesis of a first cause is surely based on the assumption that explanation must end somewhere, that an infinite series of causes is impossible and inadequate. But such a view is characteristic only of an untrained and unscientific mind. A scientist finds no difficulty in admitting an infinite series of causes. Rather according to him it is this alone which can be logically and rationally maintained. The notion of first cause is self-contradictory and meaningless. If the so-called first cause is the cause of everything else, the proper understanding of the notion of causation demands that this also must have a cause of its own. Otherwise, what it is due to? It is said that it is not due to anything; it is self-caused. But what does 'self-casualness' mean? If A is self-caused, it means that A is the cause of A. But in what circumstances A could be the cause of A? Obviously when A existed prior to A, because a cause must precede its effect. But this is self-evidently absurd, because an event cannot pre-exist itself. Thus the notion of an infinite series of causes seems more rational and justified rather than one which ends in a first cause. Why then accept a first cause? Pressing the reasonableness of the notion of infinite series of causes rather than one which ends in a first cause, Reichenbach very ably remarks, "There need not have been a first event; we can imagine that every event was preceded by an earlier event, and that time has no beginning. The infinity of time in both the directions offers no difficulties to the understanding. Infinite series without a beginning and an end have been successfully treated in mathematics; there is nothing paradoxical in them. To object that there must have been a first event, a beginning of time, is the attitude of an untrained mind. If scientific evidence is in favour of an infinite time, coming from infinity and going to infinity, logic has no objection."[37]

Here it may be re-joined by a supporter of the argument that God is not taken by the causal argument as the end of time-series such that if time-series is taken as infinite then God is not required as the last link of that series. God is really timeless and eternal and therefore, even if time-series is taken as infinite, God is still there as the first cause lying beyond the infinite time-series itself.

But the rejoinder hardly stands in the light of the clear fact that God to be the *cause* of the universe must stand in a causal, and hence in a temporal, relationship with it. If God is taken as timeless lying beyond the temporal order of the universe, then how can he be the cause of the universe? The very notion of cause demands that one who is the cause of anything must stand in a temporal relationship with it. So, God cannot be held as timeless as well as the first cause of the universe, both at the same time.

Still further criticisms may be advanced against the causal proof. It may be pointed out, for example, that even if the hypothesis of first cause is taken as granted, why only one first cause is to be taken, why not a plurality of first causes? The multiplicity of events in the world presents multiple causal series and hence there should be a multiplicity of first causes. Why only one first cause then? Why should the various chains of causation ultimately converge at only one point? It may be further pointed out that even if only one first cause of the universe is granted, it does not follow therefrom that the first cause still exists. It might have ceased to exist long ago. It is our common experience that effects endure for long, while the causes that produced them might themselves have ceased to exist. Thus the first cause might really have initiated the chain of causation present in the world, but itself it might have been dead long ago. So even if there was a God as the first cause of the universe, it is not necessary that he still exists.

However, the theologian may not find himself completely unarmed at this stage. He may come up with his defence of the causal argument by answering the above criticisms in the following manner. Like his answer to the second criticism mentioned above, the theologian may point out here that God is the first cause of its universe not only in the sense that he has created it, but also in the sense that he continually sustains and maintains it. In other words, according to him, God is not only the cause *in fieri* of the universe, rather he is also its cause in essence. By a cause *in fieri* is meant a cause which brings or helps to bring an effect into existence. By a cause in essence, on the other hand, is meant a cause which forms the very inner substance of the effect. Sometimes the two causes are different in case of an effect, but sometimes they are identical too. In case of the universe as the effect, the two causes are identical. Thus God as the first cause is both the cause *in fieri* and cause in essence. In other words, he is the originator of the universe as well as its sustainer and inner essence.

But here again the critic may ask: but who sustains and maintains God, the so-called first cause? If the whole world requires a cause in essence for its continued sustenance, there is no reason why the so-called first cause might not be requiring such a sustaining factor behind it. On what ground should we give the first cause this privileged status? If it is said that he is self-caused, then again the critic will point out that the very notion of self-causedness is absurd. It seems that even the cause-in-essence theory will work more aptly and logically by assuming the infinite series of causes rather than by taking only one self-caused first cause. Hence it cannot be maintained that there must be an ever present first cause behind the world.

As an answer to the first criticism mentioned above, the theologian may bring in what may be called his universe-as-a-whole theory. He may point out that a plurality of first causes will certainly be able to explain the multiple series of causation hat we find in the world, each first cause explaining only that particular series at the top of which it is situated. But what about the universe as a whole? God is the cause of the universe *as a whole*: he is the first cause of the entire universe, and not of any one series of causation. So, in spite of the various first causes of the various series of causation, God must be there to act as the ultimate First cause of the universe *as a whole*.

But such an argument will hardly be acceptable to the modern analytic and scientifically oriented thinker. It will be pointed out by him that the universe as a whole has no cause. The concept of causation is applicable only to particular things. or events that we observe in the universe. The concept has really been derived from there. We can meaningfully ask for the cause of one or another object or event of the universe and may, very well point to some other object or event as its cause. But to ask for the cause of the total has no meaning. As Russell says, "The whole concept of cause is one we derive from our observation of particular things: I see no reason whatever to suppose that the total has any cause whatsoever."[38] Similarly, Reichenbach remarks in this connection, "The universe as a whole has no cause, since by definition, there is nothing outside it that could be its cause. Questions of this type are empty verbalisms rather than philosophic arguments."[39] Paul Edwards tries to expose the absurdity of the notion of the cause of the universe as a whole in his own way. He seems to hold that if we point to the cause of each and every object or event of the universe by referring to some other object or event there is no sense in asking for the cause of the whole. There is nothing 'as a whole left over and above the parts. He cites a simple example in this connection. Let us suppose, he says, that a group of five Eskimos is seen standing somewhere in America.

Seeing the group there, someone wants to know as to why the group came there. After investigations he comes to the following individual explanations—Eskimo No. 1 did not enjoy the extreme cold in the polar region and decided to move to some place of warmer climate. Eskimo No. 2 was the husband of Eskimo No. 1 and he did not want to live without his wife.

Similarly, Eskimo Nos. 3, 4 and 5 came there for reasons of their own. Thus the man finds an explanation in each case and now he must understand why the group came to America. But if now he insists that he has found explanations for only the individual arrivals, and not of the entire group, then what will be our answer? According to Paul Edwards, our answer must be that the man is upset with a plainly absurd question: there is no group over and above the individual members. If he has found explanation in each case, he has found explanation in case of the whole group and there is nothing now for him to know regarding the arrival of the group. Similarly, if even after getting an explanation of the individual series of causation, the theologian raises the question of the explanation of the universe as a whole, he is raising an absurd question.[40]

But even here the theologian may try to reaffirm his position on a different plea. He may point out that events or things of the world are all contingent in nature, meaning thereby that any or all of them might well be conceived not to exist at all. Hence events of the world cannot by themselves present a sufficient explanation of their own. There must be some other being over and above the contingent objects and events of the world which could present a sufficient explanation for itself as well as for all the contingent objects of the universe. Such a being must be a necessary being, i.e., a being the non-existence of which could not even be conceived. And this necessary being is God. But such a plea really constitutes the essence of a separate argument known as the Cosmological Argument, which we shall see below.

## (c) *The Cosmological Proof*

This proof like the causal one is an *a posteriori* proof and in a way is a specific form of the causal proof itself. It constitutes. the third of the Five Ways of Aquinas and is also known as the Argument from Contingency. It tries to prove God as a necessary being, who is inevitably required for an adequate explanation of the objects of the world. The objects of the world are all contingent, meaning thereby that any or all of them could well be conceived as non-existing. The existence of none of the worldly objects seems necessary. The proof of this is that there was a time when none of the objects we now perceive existed and there will be a time in future when every one of them will cease to exist. Now, what could be the explanation of the existence of all such objects or beings in this world? Why did any of them exist at all? The contingent beings by themselves could not be their own explanations. For, as St. Aquinas argues, if everything were contingent, a situation could be conceived when nothing existed and if ever there was such a situation then nothing could ever come to be (for, nothing can come out of nothing). The final explanation of the world of contingent beings, therefore, must rest in a necessary being whose non-existence could not even be conceived. And this necessary being is. God. God, thus, as R.L. Franklin remarks, answers the final 'why?' question regarding the world.[41]

The validity of the proof mentioned above may be first of all challenged on the ground that it is perhaps not correct to say that if the things of the world are all contingent, then we might conceive a time or situation when there was nothing. Even the contingent beings might be taken as coming down one after another to us through an infinite chain of causation such that on no moment of time, there was a situation when nothing existed. Such a possibility is conceivable and therefore it does not seem correct to say time wall beings were contingent, then there must have been a time when nothing existed.

But this is hardly taken as a very important criticism of the cosmological proof. Cosmological proof does not really want to thrive on the claim that the time-series must start with a necessary being such that at no point of time a situation could be conceived when nothing existed. Its real claim seems to be that, apart from any consideration of time sequence, there is a logical connection between the necessary being and the contingent objects, such that the existence of the latter would be unintelligible without the former. A necessary being is necessary to *explain* the existence of the contingent objects. Unless there is a being whose non-existence we could not even conceive, the existence of any object in the world could not intelligibly be conceived. So, it is this logical claim of the proof which is to be examined more closely and it is really this aspect of it which has drawn greater attention of the critics. The important questions, therefore, to be considered with regard to the cosmological proof are : (1) whether the world requires an explanation of the type which cosmological proof claims to advance through the hypothesis of a necessary being, or, in other words, whether the world really remains unintelligible without the hypothesis of a necessary being and (2) whether necessary being really becomes able to explain the universe.

Criticisms of the argument, however, mainly centre round the very plausibility of the notion of a necessary being. Modern logicians point out that the notion of a necessary being is an absurd one. Nothing what is existent cannot be conceived to be non-existent. There is no logical compulsion behind the existence of any being. We have seen the clear statement of Hume in this regard in course of our consideration of the ontological argument. More recent thinkers take even a more thorough view of the notion of necessary existence and point out that it is a contradiction in terms. J.J.C. Smart, for instance, points out in one of his important essays that 'asking for a logically necessary first cause' is 'worse than asking for the moon', for, 'whereas to get the moon is only physically impossible, to get a logically necessary being is logically impossible.' In fact, as we have seen earlier in case of our treatment of the ontological argument, only propositions can be necessary or contingent in the eyes of the modern logic; beings can't be necessary or contingent. In that case, we can properly say that 'God exists' is a necessary proposition and not that God is a necessary being. But again genuinely existential propositions are not necessary. And therefore the proposition 'God exists' is either merely analytic, in which case it does not assert the real existence of God, or merely contingent—in which case God's existence does not remain necessary. So, 'necessary existence' seems to be merely an unholy combination of words. It does not mean anything.

It is obvious that the above criticism of the notion of necessary being, and through that of the cosmological argument, is based upon the supposition that in the context of the Cosmological argument, as also in the case of ontological argument, God is taken as a *logically* necessary being. Many defenders of the argument may dispute this and may point out that the Cosmological argument does not use the notion of necessary being in the sense of *logically* necessary being at all. It uses the notion only in the sense of factually necessary or ontologically necessary, meaning thereby that God is an eternal being having no beginning or end of his existence. Unlike all other beings of the world which are only temporary, God is an eternal, ever-existing being. It is never that he did not exist and it will be never that he will cease to exist. Such an eternally existing being is really or inevitably required to explain the existence of the contingent objects of the world. And it is in this sense that St. Thomas Aquinas enunciated his famous Third Way to prove the existence of a necessary being as God.

It is not clear how far the plea taken above is correct. But even if it is taken as correct, the cosmological argument does not prove to be indisputably valid. The argument, we have seen, claims to prove God as a necessary being in order to serve as an *explanation* of the contingent world. God answers the final 'why?' about the world. If God as a necessary being in the above sense were not there, the final 'why?' about the world could not be answered. And here we have to answer the two questions that we have raised above. Perhaps both these questions are to be answered negatively. Cosmological argument claims that God as a necessary being presents an answer to the question, 'Why anything in the world exists at all?' But such questions are not to be regarded as proper questions at all. The type of intelligibility regarding the universe that the cosmological proof claims to offer is not at all required. The world is not in need of such an explanation which tries to answer the question, 'why anything in the world exists at all?' Such questions are meaningless questions. The concept of explanation is applicable to only particular things that we observe in the world. It has really been derived from there. We can meaningfully ask for the explanation of one or another object of the world and we may very well point to some other object or event as its cause. But to ask for the cause or explanation of the total is non-sense. The concert of explanation is not applicable there. And if at all it is meaningful to ask about the explanation of the total, why should we not ask about the explanation of that which explains the total? The answer perhaps is that,

that is self-explained or self-explanatory. But the notion of self-explanatoryness is an absurd, meaningless notion. No being can be self-explanatory, because, for being self-explanatory it will have to pre-exist itself, which is obviously absurd. No being can have its existence prior to itself. Thus we can see that the only possible way to answer the question, 'why anything exists at all?' in a proper logical manner is by taking the final shelter in a self-explanatory being, which by its very nature is logically impossible. And this shows that the question is, logically speaking, an absurd one. As Penelhum remarks, in his important essay 'Divine Necessity', "It is absurd to ask why anything exists, because the only possible answers are in terms of the logically impossible notion of a self-explanatory being."[43] The so-called necessary being, thus, which is brought in by the cosmological argument to serve as the final explanation of the world of contingent beings would become able to do so only by reducing its own status to a logical absurdity. Nothing logically conceivable could answer the question 'why anything exists at all?'.

In a way, our second question raised above (Does God as a necessary being really become able to present the final explanation of the universe?) has also been answered in course of our answering the first question. God as a necessary being does not really become able to present the final explanation of the world, because in any attempt of doing so he himself would be reduced to a logical absurdity. We have seen above that for doing so, he will have to be self-explanatory and self-explanatoriness is logically impossible. The only other way in which we could take the necessary being as presenting the final explanation of the world is by believing somehow or other that although it is the cause of all other beings, no other being is to be found which could be taken as its cause. But what could be the ground of our such a belief? Obviously, it must either be a mere assumption or be grounded on some other independent source of knowing such as mystical intuition or something like that. But in neither case we become able to prove the necessary being to be the final explanation of the world through the cosmological argument. The cosmological argument really fails to bring in God as a necessary being to be the final explanation of the world. If, at all, it is, or may be, done, it is done on some other independent ground. Thus neither seeking for such an explanation seems to be logically sound nor God as. a necessary being becomes able to serve as such an explanation on valid logical grounds. So, we are finally compelled to conclude either with Findlay that "The modern mind feels not the faintest axiomatic force in principles which trace contingent things back to some necessarily existent source,"[44] or with T. Penelhum that "the fact that things exist cannot entail the existence of God, it could do so if God were self-explanatory. Failing this the 'why?' question would only come to a halt if we had independent reasons for holding that the being we had reached was uncaused. And it would be these independent. reasons that would bring us to theism. And it would not be atheism that *explained*. Theism cannot explain any more than atheism can."[45]

However, if we give up the claim of explanation through a necessary being, the existence of such a being as the ground and source of the world may be admitted on some other ground. That ground, as Penelhum assumes, may be one of indispensability. The word 'necessary' in the expression 'necessary being' may be taken to mean 'indispensable', i.e. 'that without which we cannot live' and in this sense the existence of a necessary being may be taken to be inevitable. But then it must be clearly understood that the hypothesis of such a necessary being does not make the concept if the world of contingent beings any more intelligible than what it would have been without such a being. In other words, such a being does not explain the existence of the world of contingent beings; it simply satisfies the finite man in making his life more easy and less problematic. So, this necessary being is not the necessary being of the cosmological proof, it is the being *felt* to be necessarily there for easing the complications of the life of the finite man.

## (d) The Teleological Proof

This proof, which is also known as the proof (or Argument) from Design (or simply Design Argument), constitutes the fifth and the last of St. Aquinas' Five Ways of proving God. It seems to be the most popular of all the proofs for the existence of the Supreme Being. It has got some such attractiveness about it that even its thorough critics like Hume have shown some praise for it. The proof takes for its starting point the allegedly obvious empirical truth that there is everywhere in the universe a sign of grand order, system and design. The universe looks like a vast machine consisting of smaller machines within it, in which the parts are all adjusted in such a beautiful manner that the overall result is a cosmos and not a chaos. Not only this, in the order of things one can also detect an organised trend towards a great purpose, end or *teleos*. What do all these speak of? They clearly speak of a great designer of supreme intelligence working behind the universe. All these cannot be there due to mere chance. It is our common experience that acts of design imply intelligent designers behind them. We can take for example the case of a watch. It is a complex structure in which the tiny parts are all adjusted and organised in a beautiful manner. Now this adjustment or organization is clearly not accidental; it is the result of a conscious effort made by an intelligent human artifact. Similarly, the act of grand design found everywhere in the universe cannot but be the act of a supreme intelligent designer. And that great intelligent designer is God.

William Paley is one of the most important modern advocates of the design argument. He actually takes the example of a watch as an act of human design and argues on the analogy of that for the existence of a supreme designer to explain the design present everywhere in the universe. According to him, the natural world is a complex mechanism in which there are numerous instances of beautiful adjustment and design. The rotation of the planets in the solar system, the regular procession of day and night and of the different seasons, the grand adaptation of the various parts of an organism, the adjustment found in one particular part itself of the organism such as the brain or the eye, are all clear examples of grand design found everywhere in the universe. Can all these be mere accidental? Certainly not. They all clearly speak of a supreme intelligent designer behind them who is called God, the Supreme Being. And thus the Supreme Being exists.

In spite of the apparent attractiveness that the argument has about it, it does not prove very sound on logical examination. The most obvious weakness lies in the fact that it does not really prove a God, rather it simply proves a designer, an artificer working behind the world. Designing implies nothing more than merely rearranging certain materials already given. If God is taken as a mere designer in this sense, he is certainly not that God of theism who is taken as the infinite, omnipotent *creator* of the universe. If certain materials exist beyond God from beforehand and God is there simply to rearrange them in an attractive fashion, then such a God becomes limited and finite and no longer remains God at all in the real sense of the term. So the design argument, if at all it becomes able to prove anything, becomes able to prove only a designer of a limited capacity and not a supreme, all-powerful creator God.

Secondly, the very empirical hypothesis on which the argument is based (that there is design, order, adjustment and organisation everywhere in the world) may be disputed. It may be pointed out that side by side with the examples of adjustment and organisation, there are in the universe examples of mal-adjustment, disharmony and disorder too. The world does not look to be a sphere of unqualified design such that as the cause of it we are constrained to postulate a designer. Even if it is accepted that the world is full of design, adjustment and organisation, it does not seem to follow necessarily therefrom that it is an act of an intelligent designer. The designs found in different organisms, in various animals and plants may all be due to a gradual process of evolution or due to some such other process of natural adaptation. That the design present in the world is the result of an intelligent planning by a conscious designer may be taken as the only one hypothesis out of the various others that may be brought in to explain the phenomenon. And therefore the fact of design does not necessarily prove the existence of an intelligent designer.

More logical criticism, however, still awaits the argument. It can be seen that the nerve of the argument lies in an analogy drawn between ordinary acts of human design and the design found in the universe at large. Just as a watch or a house is an act of design, similarly the entire universe seems to be an act of design. We know that behind the act of design found in the watch or the house, there is an intelligent human designer. On analogy, therefore, we may infer that behind the design found in the universe also, there is an intelligent designer quite proportionate to the act of design that the whole universe manifests. The designer behind the world must possess infinitely more power and greater amount of intelligence than the ordinary human designer. Now here apart from a point of doubt whether the argument really becomes able to prove an *infinitely* powerful and intelligent being as the designer of the world, we shall like to take up the more logical point whether the analogy drawn here is apt, perfect and good. Hume has dealt at length on this point in his book *Dialogues Concerning Natural Religion* and there he seems to take the view that the conclusion of the design argument is based on an imperfect and bad analogy. He points out there that the analogy drawn between a house or a watch on the one side and the universe on the other is not so perfect and good that any conclusion about the latter may be drawn on the basis of the former. "But surely you will not affirm, that the universe bears such a resemblance to a house, that we can with the same certainty infer a similar cause, or the analogy here is entire and perfect. The dissimilitude is so striking, that the utmost you can here pretend to is a guess, a conjecture, a presumption concerning a similar cause ......"[48] And a mere guess is certainly not a proof. So the weak points of similarity between a house or a watch on the one hand and the entire universe on the other do not warrant one to draw any conclusion about the latter on the basis of the former. "Does not the great disproportion", asks Hume, "bar all comparison and inference?"

Further, analogies are drawn between such empiricals about both (or all) of which some important points in which they resemble are known. We can draw an analogy between a house and a watch because both of them are facts of the empirical world and we have seen and known many things about their origin, functioning etc. Here, on the basis of one, we may reasonably draw some inference about the other. But to draw an analogy between a watch and the entire universe is very unusual, unconventional and unbecoming. We have seen many things about watch but we have hardly seen or known anything about the origin of our universe. Had there been other universes like our own and we had experienced that they had been designed by some designer, then by a comparison between our present universe and those universes, we could have reasonably inferred on analogy that our present universe also must have been designed by a designer. But seeing about a watch that it has a designer, we can with no propriety infer on the basis of analogical reasoning that the universe also must have a designer. The comparison here is not at all apt and so the analogy employed here is a kind of bad analogy.[46]

One more general point may be added here by way of showing the weakness of the argument. Even if it is accepted that the analogy employed here has some force, it may at least be said on the basis of the argument that there is *probably* a designer behind the universe. For, we know that conclusions based on analogical reasonings are only probable. So in no case the argument is able to prove with certainty that there is a God behind the world, if at all the mere designer claim to be proved by the argument be taken as God.

## (e) The Moral Proof

This proof has two forms. In one of its forms, it seems not to be a proof at all, rather a mere persuasive plea to render the assumption of God's existence somehow justifiable. This sort of persuasive argument seems involved in Kant's *Critique of Practical Reason*. It is well known that in his *Critique of Pure Reason* Kant criticised the rational proofs to demonstrate that pure reason was unable to prove God. However, he tried to impress in his *Practical Reason* that what could not be demonstrated on pure reason could be well postulated on practical reason. Reason could not prove God, but still there must be a God to meet the demands of morality. If God is not supposed to exist, moral life cannot bear its full significance. Even if reason is unable to prove God, morality requires him as its very presupposition. Morality to be a meaningful pursuit must have happiness as its final reward. But we find in common life that even the most virtuous sometimes greatly suffer. If this is taken as the final end of the show, morality can hardly have any real significance in man's life. It is only when man gets the assurance that there is a God behind the world as its moral governor who will someday or other, either in the present life or in a life beyond, will reconcile virtue with happiness, that he gets the consolation for his moral sacrifices and continues to be moral in spite of all odds and sufferings. Thus, if morality is to play a significant role in human life, God must be presupposed to work as a moral governor behind the apparent show of the world.

In brief, this is Kant's moral proof. It is clear that properly speaking it is not a proof at all. God is not *proved* here, rather what is attempted to be shown here is that, if God is not taken as existing, morality cannot have a real significance in man's life. There is no need therefore to go into the logical merits and demerits of the alleged proof.

In more modern times, however, the moral proof has been presented in a form which really comes out to be proof for the existence of the Supreme Being. The proof has been presented in an importantly recognised manner by Hastings Rashdall and W.R. Sorley. It starts from the premise of the objectivity of moral law (or laws) and moral values and proves God as the ground of these laws and values. It is argued that the objective moral laws and moral values involved in the very structure and go of the universe cannot admit of a naturalistic explanation, because their nature has hardly any affinity with any of the natural phenomena. Some conscious mind must therefore be the ground of these moral laws and values. The values and the moral laws have a spiritual affiliation about them and therefore they have affinity with mind and consciousness. But again any finite mind cannot be the ground of these laws and values, because in that case they will be merely relative and subjective and not objective and absolute. The objective nature of these values, therefore, demands that they must be grounded in an infinite, absolute or objective mind. And that is God. Thus God is proved here to be the ground of objective moral laws and values. As Rashdall argues in his book *The Theory of Good and Evil*, "An absolute Moral Law or moral ideal cannot exist in material things. And it does not exist in the mind of this or that individual. Only if we believe in the existence of a Mind for which the true moral ideal is already in some sense real, a Mind which is the source of whatever is true in our own moral judgments, can we rationally think of the moral ideal as no less real than the world itself. Only so can we believe in an absolute standard of right and wrong which is as independent of this or that man's actual ideas and actual desires as the facts of material nature. The belief in God, though not a postulate of there being any such thing as Morality at all, is the logical presupposition of an 'objective' or absolute Morality. A moral ideal can exist nowhere and no how but in a mind; an absolute moral ideal can exist only in a Mind from which all Reality is derived. Our moral ideal can claim only in so far as it can rationally be regarded as the revelation of a moral ideal eternally existing in the mind of God."[47]

The argument is clearly based on two assumptions, both of which are questionable. The two assumptions are: (1) The moral law or laws and the moral values are objective and (2) They do not admit of any explanation other than that they are grounded in some Divine mind. That there are uniform moral laws (like the natural laws) somehow involved in the go of the universe and that there are objective moral values are both disputed and uncertain propositions. The universe does not as clearly and unambiguously manifest the working of some moral law or laws behind it as it manifests the working of natural laws. Then again it is very much disputed amongst thinkers whether moral values like those of right, good, etc. are objective or subjective. Both the views have arguments and theories in favour of them.

Mr. Sorley, of course, argues strongly in his book *Moral Values and the Idea of God*[48] for the objectivity of moral values, but there are no less strong arguments in favour of the subjectivity of moral values advanced by thinkers such as Perry, Ayer, Stevenson etc. The moral proof is, therefore, based on a very dubious proposition, the veracity of which has not been proved so far.

Further, this is also not shown that a Divine mind is necessary to explain the objectivity of moral law or moral values, if at all they are taken as objective. Advocates of the autonomy of morals have much disputed the authenticity and desirability of any religious morality. Even if the moral values do not admit of any naturalistic explanation, it is not necessary that a Divine mind is brought in to explain them. These values may well be autonomous and self-dependent. Similar may be the case with moral law or laws. The Hindu belief in the law of *Karma*, which is regarded as a pervasive law, as much works in the context of an atheistic system like *Mimansa* or *Samkhya* as it works in the context of the theistic systems. No God is necessarily required to serve as the ground of the moral law. The moral law can very well be autonomous and self-dependent.

Hence it seems that the moral proof also like all other proofs fails to prove the existence of God.

## ii. Conclusion

We have thus made a survey of the important rational proofs for the existence of God. We have seen that none of the proofs is able on valid logical grounds to prove the existence of such a being. Certain other arguments based on the occurrence of specific experiences or events (such as, Argument from Religious Experience, about which we have said something towards the beginning, or Argument from Miracles) are also sometimes advanced to prove the existence of God. But really speaking they are not to be taken as proofs, at least not rational proofs, which we have liked to take here for our consideration. In fact, even of the five proofs that we have considered above, only two-the ontological and the cosmological-seem worthy to be taken as proofs in the strict sense of the term 'proof'. The former is a real demonstrative proof starting from an *a priori* premise concerning the idea of the concept of God and deducing therefrom through a *Reductio* the necessary existence of God. The latter although starts from an *a posteriori* premise is still to be regarded as a logical proof, because it is based on the claim of a logical connection between the world and the necessary being as its ground. The other proofs seem merely to be attempts at adducing evidences based on empirical grounds to render the theistic hypothesis more probable than the atheistic one. They cannot, strictly speaking, be taken as *proofs* for the existence of the Supreme Being. In any case, all the proofs miserably fail in their mission. Every one of them contains sufficient flaw within it which helps the unbeliever sustain his doubts about the existence of a Supreme Being unmitigated and unabated. The so-called proofs, we have seen, really fail to prove the existence of God.

In fact, the very idea of proving God through rational arguments seems basically misconceived. For, such arguments will be either deductive or non-deductive (inductive, analogical etc.) and none of them on analysis seems capable of proving the truth of a proposition which asserts the existence of God. Deductive arguments of the strict demonstrative form starting from purely *a priori* premises are hardly able to do so, because from premises stating merely certain relations between ideas or concepts, a truly existential proposition stating the real existence of God can hardly be derived. Only such arguments of the deductive form may be able to prove the existence of God which start from factual premises. But wherefrom such factual premises are to be got? Obviously from our experience of the world. But will there be conceivably any proposition or propositions derived from our experience of the finite world which will entail a proposition asserting the existence of a being which is by its very nature non-empirical and infinite? Perhaps not. And so, deductive reasonings seem unable to establish the existence of God.

Non-deductive reasonings of any sort will definitely start from factual premises based on our experience of the world and try to prove on the evidence of their truth the truth of proposition about God's existence. But for reasons mentioned above in connection with the latter kind of deductive reasoning, such proofs are also bound to fail. A proposition asserting the existence of a non-empirical and infinite being cannot be proved on the evidence of premises concerning facts of ordinary experience. It may, however, be pointed out here that such premises will certainly not entail or form conclusive proof for the existence of God, but they may very well form probable evidence for the same. As a matter of fact, non-deductive reasonings never claim certainty, they only claim probability of truth. But we can see that on closer examination, even claims probability in the present case seem to be a dubious hypothesis. The claims of probability made by inductive or analogical reasonings are justified only when on the basis of premises about some empiricals, they derive conclusions about other empiricals, which may for the time being be unexperienced, but are in principle experienceable and are things of the same empirical order. But there is hardly any probability of truth in a conclusion which asserts a fact of a completely different nature and order from those the assertion of which has formed the content of the premises from which it has been derived. Had there been certain other universes like our own and about some of them we had experienced that such and such were the case, then with ample scope for probability, we could derive about our own universe that that might be the case about it also. But by seeing things about finite events within our own universe, we can with no real plausibility derive anything about the whole of it. As Hume very aptly puts the matter in the mouth of Philo in his *Dialogues*, "When two species of objects have always been observed to be conjoined together, I can *infer*, by custom, the existence of one wherever I see the existence of the other: and this I call an argument from experience. But how can this argument have place, where the objects, as in the present case, are single, individual, without parallel or specific resemblance, may be difficult to explain ........ To ascertain this reasoning, it was requisite, that we had the experience of the origin of worlds; and it is not sufficient surely, that we have seen ships and cities arise from human art and contrivance......"[49] Non-deductive reasonings also therefore seem to fail in the present case even in the fulfilment of their moderate mission.

It seems very reasonable therefore to conclude that rational arguments cannot prove God. Howsoever emotive the following lines of Kierkegaard may seem to be, they still seem to have a real force behind them, "The idea of demonstrating that this unknown something (God) exists could scarcely suggest itself to reason. For if God does not exist it would of course be impossible to prove it: and if he does exist, it would be folly to attempt it."[50]

## REFERENCES

1. St. Anselm, *Proslogian*, Chapter II.
2. N. Malcolm, 'Anselm's Ontological Arguments' in *The Philosophical Review*, January 1960.
3. St. Anselm, *Proslogian*, Chapter III.
4. *Meditations*, V.
5. Immanuel Kant, *Critique of Pure Reason*, tr. N. Kemp Smith (London, 1929), p. 502.
6. *Ibid.*, pp. 504-5.
7. In an essay 'Is Existence a Predicate?' first published in *Aristotelian Society*, Suppl. Vol. XV, 1936 and reprinted in A. Flew's (ed.) *Logic and Language*, Second series.
8. An idea can be formed by the following list—
   a. A.J. Ayer, *Language, Truth and Logic*, p. 43.
   b. John Wisdom, *Interpretation & Analysis* (London, 1931), p. 62.
   c. W.F. Kneale, 'Is Existence a Predicate?' in *Aristotelian Society*, Suppl. Vol. XV, 1936.
   d. John E. Smith, *Reason & God* New Haven & London: Yale Univ. Press, 1961), pp. 122-23.
   e. B. Russell, *Logic & Knowledge* ed. by R. Marsh (George Allen & Unwin, 1964), p. 232ff.
   f. J. Shaffer, 'Existence, Predication and the Ontological Argument' in *Mind*, July 1962 and

reprinted in John Hick and A. Mc Gill (ed). *The Many-Faced Argument* (Macmillan, 1968).

    g.   G. Nakhnikian & Wesley C. Salmon, "Exists" as a Predicate' in *Philosophical Review*, Vol. 66, 1957.

    h.   F.P. Alston, 'The Ontological Argument revisited' in *Philosophical Review*, Vol. 69, 1960.

9. B. Russell, *op. cit,,* p. 233.

10. J. Shafter, *op. cit.*, p. 310, in *Mind*, July, 1962 and p. 229 in John Hick & McGill's *The Many-Faced Argument*.

11. G. Nakhnikian & Wesley C. Salmon, *op. cit.*, p. 542.

12. J. Shaffer, *op. cit.*, in *Mind*, July, 1962, p. 323.

13. *Ibid.*, p. 325.

14. Immanuel Kant, *op. cit.*, p. 505.

15. In an essay entitled "Can God's Existence be Disproved?" included in A. Flew & A.C. Mc Intyre (ed.), *New Essays in Philosophical Theology* (S.C.M. London, 1955).

16. *Ibid.*, p. 55

17. *Ibid.*, p. 54.

18. *Ibid.*, p. 54.

19. .. that all existential propcsitions are contirgent in, properly understocd, a theory about empirical propcsition; and it does not in the slightest follow fiom the view that all empirical existential propositions are contingent that there may not be some other class of propositions which are not to be given such an analysis." G.E. Hughes in his share on 'Can God's Existence be Disproved ?' included in A. Flew & A.C. Mc Inty"e (ed.) *New Essay* etc., p. 60.

20. "I believe we may rightly take the existence of those religious systems of thought in which Ged figures as a necessary being to be a disproof of the dogma, affirmed by Hume and others, that no existential proposition can be necessary." N. Malcolm in his essay 'Anselm's Ontological arguments' first published in *Philosophical Review*, Vol. 69, 1960 and reprinted in John Hick & A. McGill (ed.) *The Many-Faced Argument*. The passage has been quoted here from John Hick etc. (ed.) book, p. 15.

21. "The necessity of God's Existence is not the same as the necessity of a logical implication ...It is a property ascribed to God, not a property of our assertions about God. To maintain that the ascription of such a property is logically absurd is to confuse the necessity of God's Being with the necessity of our thinking about it." A.C.A. Rainer in his share on Can God's Existence be Disproved ?' in A. Flew and A.C. Mc Intyre (ed.), *op. cit.*, p. 68.

22. "He (Findlay) takes for granted an unfortunate and untypical assimilation of this necessity (the necessity of God) to the necessity of propositions about it." P.E. Hutchings, Necessary Being and Some Types of Tautology' in *Philosophy*, January, 1964, p. 9.

23. R.E. Allen, 'The Ontological Argument', *Philosophical Review*, January, 1961, p. 59.

24. Findlay, *op. cit.*, p. 73.

25. N. Malcolm, *op. cit*.

26. S. Hartshorne, *The Logic of Perfection*, (Lasalle, Open Court Pub. Co., 1962) Chap II, a portion of which is included in John Hick & A. McGill, *op.cit*

27. John Hick & A. McGill, op.cit p. 336

28. N. Malcolm, *op. cit.*, in John Hick & A. McGill (ed.), *op. cit.*, pp. 308-309.

29. *Ibid.*, p. 309.

30. Charles Hartshorne, *op. cit*, in John Hick & A. Mill (d.), *op cit.*, p. 335.

31. David Hume, *Dialogues Concerning Natural Religion*, Part IX.

32. John Hick, A Critique of the "Second Argument", included in John Hick & A. McGill's, *op. cit.*, p. 348.

33. *Ibid*.

34. *Ibid.*, p. 343.

35. As a matter of fact, there have been many reactions against Malcolm's defence of Anselm's ontological argument. A number of reactions were published in the very next issue of the Journal *Philosophical Review*) in which Malcolm's essay was originally published. The reactions published in the said issue of the Journal include the following-

   a. R.E. Allen, The Ontological Argument', pp. 56-65.

   b. R. Abelson, 'Not Necessarily', pp. 67-84.

   c. T. Penelhum, 'On the Second Ontological Argument', pp. 85-92.

   d. A. Plantinga, A Valid Ontological Argument', pp. 93-101.

   e. Paul Henlle, 'Uses of Ontological Argument', pp. 102-109.

   f. G.B. Mathews, On Conceivability in Anselm & Malcolm', pp. 110-11. All in *Philosophical Review*, Vol. 70, January, 1961.

36. Findlay, *Ibid.*, p. 47.

37. H. Reichenbach, *The Rise of Scientific Philosophy* (University of California Press, 1951), pp. 207-8.

38. From a debate between Russell and Copelston, reprinted in Russell's *Why I am not a Christian* and other Essays (George Allen & Unwin, 1957), pp. 151-52.

39. H. Reichenbach, *op. cit.*, p. 208.

40. *A Modern Introduction to Philosophy*, ed. by P. Edwards & A. Pap., p. 454.

41. R.L, Franklin, "Necessary Being' in *Australasian Journal of Philosophy*, August, 1967.

42. J.J.C. Smart, "The Existence of God', in *New Essays in Philosophical Theology*, p. 39.

43. T. Penelhum, 'Divine Necessity' in *Mind*, April, 1960, p. 182.

44. J.N, Findlay, *op. cit.*, p. 54.

45. T. Penelhum, *op. cit.*, p. 182.

46. One may see here A. Pap, *Elements of Analytic Philosophy* (New York, Macmillan, 1949), Chapter IX, Sec. C.

47. H. Rashdall, *The Theory of Good and Evil* (1907), Vol. II, p. 212.

48. Cambridge University Press, 1919.

49. David Hume, *Dialogues Concerning Natural Religion*, Part II.

50. S. Kierkagaard, "The Absolute Paradox' in John Hick's (ed.) *The Existence of God*, p. 212.

## Section III
## FAITH

The term 'faith' is very slippery in nature and it has been variously understood in philosophy. Very frequently it is taken as something purely subjective denoting some specific kind of feeling or disposition. It is therefore sometimes defined as 'assurance of the things hoped for'. Tennant takes faith as an 'unverifiable hope'. Such conceptions of faith clearly indicate that faith is a state of hope for the things unseen. It is believing in certain things whose being or existence cannot be verified, but which somehow give the believer a hope of being sustained in moments of despair and anxiety. Such a conception of faith is obviously purely subjective and it has no objective root. But there are others, mostly theologians, who take faith as a genuinely cognitive state of mind that gives us knowledge about some objective reality. Faith in this sense is a special kind of knowledge. In the Biblical sense it is generally understood as a human 'response' to the Divine revelation. It is believed that God sometimes reveals himself through the specific events of history and faith is nothing but the apprehension or cognition of God through such events. There is a trend in Christianity which believes that the entire human history, i.e. the entire cosmos, is a revelation of God and to see or to interpret the cosmos in this light is faith. In any case, however, faith in the sense of a human response to the divine revelation is cognitive in nature and consists in experiencing God in the general or specific events of history. There are other conceptions (e.g. the Tillichian conception that faith is a state of being ultimately concerned) of faith also, but we are concerned here mainly with such conceptions which take faith as genuinely cognitive, because it is one such a concept of faith that the factuality of God-statements can be based. There-fore, we will confine ourselves here to the exposition and. assessment of only such views.

Theologians have sometimes tried to defend the factual status of religious statements by an appeal to faith. They point out that God is by his very nature mysterious, infinite and unique and therefore it is impossible to know him in ordinary ways. Even religious experiences are unable to give a doubtless and a true picture of God because infinite characteristics cannot be the objects of religious experience.[1] "It therefore seems more in accordance with the nature of the subject-matter to begin by noting that there is what we may call the circle of faith in which it seems evident that God exists, that the *question* as to whether he exists does not even arise."[2] There have been thinkers from the very old tradition to defend the objective status of God on faith. But here in our present discussion, we shall take up only two very recent attempts made in the characteristic contemporary analytic spirit by two eminent thinkers-John Hick and John Ballie—to defend the factual status of religious statements.

Hick points out that the religious man so often reports of his seeing or being aware of a God through his ordinary experiences themselves and not "in isolation from all other objects of experience."[3] It is this act of seeing or 'knowing' a God by the religious man through the ordinary experiences themselves which Hick seems to term as faith. Now, what Hick tries to do as his first attempt to give the statements of religion the same (or similar) factual status as that of ordinary factual or scientific statements is to show that the pattern of the religious man's (what he calls) 'cognition' or 'knowledge' of God is basically the same as that of our ordinary cognitions of worldly objects. Or, to quote his own words, what he is anxious to show is that "While the object of religious knowledge is unique, its basic epistemological pattern is that of all our knowing."[4] This, again, Hick tries to do on the argument that in every act of cognition there are two things— 'significance' and 'interpretation'. By 'significance' he seems to mean the data of our cognition, and by 'interpretation' he means the sense that is sought into the data by the cognisor. Now, he points out that in both the cognitions, religious and sense-empirical, the data are the same. What differs is the interpretation. In both the cognitions an act of interpretation is there, but it is not the same in the two cases. When interpreted in one way, we see through the data a world of physical objects, but when interpreted in another way, we see through the same data something more than the mere world: we see a world created and sustained by a God. The first, we can say, is open to everyone, but the second is not so. But Hick will point out here that the second is also equally open to everyone; it is only not sought by everyone. As he says, " ... the data of religious experience are for the most part the same as those through which we know physical objects and other human beings. They consist in the ordinary human experience which is common to believers and non-believers-together with further experiences which are open to everyone but which are not in fact sought by everyone."[5]

However, there is, according to Hick, a uniqueness about the data which constitute 'significance' for religious cognition as compared to those which constitute 'significance' for our ordinary cognitions of physical objects. The 'significance' in the former case is constituted for us by the data presented by the world as a whole, while the significance in the latter case is constituted by the piecemeal sections of the world. The religious interpretation is thus a 'total interpretation' i.e., an interpretation made out of the data presented in one's experience of the world as a whole. To quote Hick's own word in this connection, "The primary locus of religious significance is the believer's experience as a whole. The basic act of interpretation which reveals to him the religious significance of life is a uniquely 'total interpretation'...."[6] Thus religious cognition or 'faith-apprehension', as Hick sometimes calls it, is nothing but a seeing through of a divine trend or divine presence in the objects of the world and such an apprehension or seeing through comes by an act of 'total interpretation' of the data presented to the religious man by the world as a whole.

Anyway, basically, according to Hick, the procedure involved in the act of knowing God is not different from that involved in knowing physical objects-at least not different from the knowing that gives us the belief that there is an objective physical world (the entire physical environment and not this or that physical object) before us. Sometimes, through the data we see a bare physical world, and sometimes through the same data we see a divine presence, a God. It is however a mystery how one sees a world of physical environment through the data and again sometimes sees a God mediating through it. In both the cases the mystery persists and the man simply finds himself interpreting the data present in his conscious experience in one way or the other. As Hick says, "There is in cognition of every kind an unresolved mystery. The knower-known relationship is in the last analysis *sui generis*: the mystery of cognition persists at the end of every enquiry-its persistence does not prevent us from cognizing. We cannot explain, for example, how we are conscious of sensory-phenomena as constituting an objective physical environment; we just find ourselves interpreting the data of our experience in this way.... The same is true of the apprehension of God. The theistic believer cannot explain *how* he knows the divine presence to be mediated through his human experience. He just finds himself interpreting his experience in this way."[7]

It is in this way that Hick tries to show that faith (the act of seeing God through the ordinary human experience) has the same epistemological pattern as that of knowledge (the act of seeing a physical world through the same ordinary experience). Through this Hick certainly wants to show that the cognition of God by the religious man is as much a genuine case of cognition' or 'knowledge' as that of the physical world by the ordinary man. And hence the statements about God have the same (or similar) factual status as that of the statements about the physical world. But in seeing such a similarity between the two cognitions, we have to remark very oddly, Hick either fails to see some of the vital differences between the two forms of cognition or, if he sees them as he actually does,[8] he fails to appreciate them properly. His attempt to give religious knowledge the same factual status as that of ordinary factual or scientific knowledge does not seem to succeed on examination. It is only by seeing the two cognitions on a superficial level that one can mark similarities, but if one goes deeper, he can see that the differences are more vital than the similarities.

The very first thing that should occur to us is that the physical world is visible to all of us, but God is not so visible. There is, no doubt, a superficial and sweeping similarity between the process of knowing the world and that of knowing God in as much as in both the cases there is a 'significance' (and the significance for the most part is the same in both the cases)[9] and an act of 'interpretation' involved. But there is a great difference involved in the act of interpretation itself which is sufficient for bringing the essential difference between the two acts of cognition. The data presented by the physical world are easily interpreted by every normal person to constitute what is called an objective physical world, but only some interpret them in the way which makes them believe that there is a God present in the world. This shows that the interpretation in the first case is independent of any personal involvement or prior commitment but the interpretation in the second case is dependent upon some prior commitment or some specific kind of faith or trust. A religious interpretation of the data is not possible unless the man concerned looks to it with a specific attitude, with a specific conviction. In other words, in the cognition of God through the data, the man himself is somehow significantly involved in the situation; he is looking to the situation with a specific concern. But a purely physical or naturalistic interpretation of the world does not require any such commitment. The personality of the observer or the interpreter is detached from the acts of interpretation in this case.[10] Hick says that the knower-known relationship is in both the cases a mystery. The knower does not know how he is knowing what he is knowing. He simply finds him interpreting the data that way. It is a fact that the believer simply finds himself in the presence of God mediated through his ordinary experience, while a non-believer finds himself in the presence of a bare world. But for the philosopher the thing does not remain so much a mystery when he finds that the perception of the world is, more or less, coercive and universal while the perception of God is not so. At least this much of the mystery is certainly unveiled that the believer is looking to the data with a specific conviction, while the so-called non-believer has no special convictions: he is looking to the data unconcerned and in a neutral way. Hick himself is conscious enough to see the difference between the two cognitions in the above light when he recognises that while sense-perception is coercive in nature, religious perception is not so, but then in spite of that, peculiarly enough, he concludes that they do not debar religious cognition, to be similar in nature to that of ordinary cognition.

Not only this, Hick sees that to give religious statements a full factual status like that of ordinary factual or scientific statements, it is necessary that they may be verifiable and falsifiable with reference to some empirical data. If religious knowledge is to be put at a par with scientific knowledge, the former must also be verifiable and falsifiable like the latter. Hick fully realises the force of the demand and he actually proceeds to prove a verifiability and falsifiability of religious cognition in his own characteristic way (by an appeal to eschatological experience) which we will see in a later section. We will find there that despite that attempt also he fails to save the genuine factual status of religious statements.

Another contemporary theologian who wants to save the factual status of religious statements on the ground of faith is John Ballie. Ballie is a Barthian with certain reservations and therefore he does not allow the presence of God to the believer to be mediated through ordinary human experience. God directly reveals himself in man's consciousness and the apprehension of this revelation by him is faith according to him. Of course, this revelation has not got any forced access upon man. It is open to those alone or it is apprehended by those alone who are tied to it by a prior sense of commitment (and here in recognising the human role in divine revelation, Ballie seems to differ from Barth). Hence Ballie defines faith as 'apprehension through commitment'.[11] Nevertheless (i.e., in spite of the fact that a commitment is necessary on man's part to see God), God is perfectly objective. His existence does not depend upon human cognition or apprehension of him. The apprehension itself is produced in us by him in the same way in which our ordinary sense-experience is produced in us by objects lying outside us. As he himself says, "Faith is experience, but like all other experiences it is determined for us and produced in us by something not ourselves. We cannot make ourselves believe and we should not try. If it is veridical at all, faith is the gift of God."[12]

Thus, like Hick, Ballie also tries to give the faith-apprehension of God the same cognitive (or knowledge) status as that of ordinary sense-apprehension and hence the religious statements the same factual status as that of ordinary factual statements. The difference lies only in the approach. Hick approaches the problem from the side of the cognisor or the knower and Ballie from the side of the cognised or the known. But like Hick he also forgets that whereas sense-cognition occurs to all of us, faith-apprehension does not occur to all. If the objects of faith-apprehension would have been as objective and real as that of the ordinary sense-cognition, then like the latter, the former should also occur to all. Ballie himself recognises that for a religious cognition a prior commitment is necessary on the part of the man. Such a specific prior commitment, on the other hand, is not required in the case of ordinary cognitions. They occur in a coercive way even to a neutral, non-committed observer. How can then a cognition which necessarily requires a prior commitment on the part of the cognisor can be as objective as that which does not necessitate any such commitment?[13] How can God claim the same objective status as that of physical objects, if the very precondition of knowing him is a prior commitment?

Not only this. Like Hick, Ballie also realises that to give God a full objective status and hence to give religious statements the same factual status as that of ordinary factual or scientific statements, it is necessary that the former kind of statements must also be verifiable and falsifiable like the latter ones. And he actually tries to prove such a verifiability and falsifiability of religious statements. He argues that each factual statement is verified and falsified with reference to its 'primary apprehension', i.e. with reference to the apprehension or cognition through which the statement occurs to man. Ordinary factual statements are verified and falsified with reference to their sphere of primary apprehension, the sense-experience. Similarly, the religious statements are also to be verified and falsified with reference to their primary apprehension, the faith-apprehension. As he says, "If .... all theoretical judgments are to be verified by a return to the area of primary apprehension (or experience) which first suggested them, then our answer (to the question, how are theological judgments verified?) must be that theological judgments can be verified only by a return to the area of primary apprehension which we call faith."[14]

But here again, we will have to point out that although Ballie draws a point-to-point comparison between the verifiability of ordinary factual statements and that of religious statements with a clear sense of giving the latter the same factual status as that of the former, he forgets that there is a difference in a very important respect between the verifiability of the two kinds of statements and in view of that difference, the latter cannot have the same factual status as that of the former. The former, i.e. the ordinary factual statements are verifiable by all, whereas the latter are verifiable by only those few who are bound by a common commitment. The point we have seen in much details while seeing the claims of religious experience and the same will apply here also. Therefore, we need not go into them again.

And hence, we have found that attempts made by an appeal to faith by Hick and Ballie have failed to save the genuine objective status of religious statements. And really speaking, any such attempt is bound to fail, because faith-apprehension necessarily implies some kind of prior conviction, trust or commitment on the part of the believer[15] and a cognition which necessarily requires a prior commitment cannot be genuinely objective. To talk of genuine objectivity, of genuine knowledge-claim, of the verifiability and falsifiability of one's statements like ordinary (factual statements and at the same time of the necessity of a prior commitment to have such knowledge or objectivity is like trying both to have a cake and eat it at the same time, which is impossible.

## REFERENCES

1. John Hick, 'Meaning & Truth in Religion' in *Religious Experience & Truth* (Oliver & Boyed, 1962, New York, University Press, 1961), edited by Sydney Hook, p. 206.

2. *Ibid.*, p. 209.

3. John Hick, *Faith & Knowledge* (Ithaca, Cornel University Press, 1957), p. 109.

4. *Ibid.*, p. 111.

5. John Hick, *Faith & Philosophers* (London, Macmillan, 1964), edited by John Hick, p.243.

6. John Hick, *Faith & Knowledge*, p. 127.

7. *Ibid.*, p. 132.

8. John Hick, *Faith and Philosophers*, p. 245.

9. However, if we take into consideration the knowledge of individual objects, even the 'significance' is not the same, because in this case the experience of piecemeal sections of the world forms the significance' while in case of religious cognition the experience of the world as a whole forms the 'significance'.

10. The point is, however, controversial. It is generally argued that even in scientific cognitions, there is a subjective personal element involved.

11. John Ballie, *The Sense of the Presence of God*, Gifford Lectures, 1961-62 (Oxford University Press, 1962), p. 90.

12. *Ibid.*, pp. 65-66.

13. The point, as we have already conceded, is not free from controversies. Scientific cognitions are also said to be based on certain commitments. But we can see that such commitments in case of scientific statements are of so general a nature that for practical purposes they may be neglected.

14. John Ballie, *ibid.*, p. 67 on falsifiability specifically, pp. 69ff.

15. Hick, perhaps, openly hesitates to admit it because he believes that ".... the faith as trust presupposes faith as cognition"' (*Faith & Knowledge*, Introduction, p. XII). But really speaking, as we shall see towards the end, that faith as cognition itself as much presupposes faith as trust as the latter presupposes the former. Without a prior trust or commitment, there can't be faith-apprehension. Hick himself in a way implies it when he takes both naturalism and theism as 'total interpretations'. Unless certain prior convictions are there, how are different total interpretations made out of the same data or 'significance'? Hick in a way admits it also there where he makes a distinction between coercive and non-coercive cognition and while putting sense-perception under the former category he puts the religious cognitions under the latter.

## Section IV
## ATTRIBUTES OF GOD AND THE QUESTION OF FACTUALITY OF RELIGIOUS BELIEF

We have said earlier that the question of the factuality of religious belief is a question not only of the existence of God or in other words, not only of the applicability of the subject-term 'God' to some real fact, but also of the nature of the attributes of God, or in other words, of the fact whether the words used in the predicate of the religious statements really and meaningfully convey some information about, or describe some real features of, the subject. Thus, besides seeing the question of the meaning and factual applicability of the term 'God', contemporary philosophical theology also dwells much on examining the meaning of the attributes and their ability of meaningfully describing some real state-of-affairs. Before closing our chapter on the factuality of religious belief, therefore, we will have to consider the different aspects and the different views relating to the nature and factual meaningfulness of the various attributes given to God.

Of the various attributes and characteristics given to God, the two types of attributes known as metaphysical and ethical have been mostly emphasized by natural theology. The metaphysical attributes given to God are the attributes of omnipotence, omniscience, and omnipresence, and the ethical ones are those of benevolence, justice, love etc. Besides these, God is regarded as the creator of the world and is also taken to sustain it by acting through it. Now, the natural theologians from the very old days have taken these attributes as faithful descriptions of God. They take God as an objective reality existing somehow and somewhere and the attributes given to him as the descriptions of his nature. God is the creator and sustainer of the whole world and therefore he must be something infinite and possess infinite characters. He is all-powerful (omnipotent), all-knowing (omniscient) and all-present (omnipresent). Again, he is perfectly good, loving and just in nature.

But most of the contemporary philosophical theology which dwells in a refutation of the factual, descriptive or informative nature of religious statements points out by analysis that the attributes given to God cannot have any factual and descriptive meaning. Properly analysed and seen, it points out, the attributes do not come to be meaningful descriptions of an objective reality. They are either factually vacuous or self-contradictory in nature. The attributes seen again in the light of God's relationship with the world, which he is said to have created and which he also sustains, are mutually incompatible with each other. They show a self-evident contradiction in God's nature and sometimes even his non-existence. Further, about some attributes given to God, it is not even clear in what sense they are to be understood and applied to God. Taking all these facts into consideration, it is pointed out that as descriptions of the nature of an objective reality the predicates given to God do not carry any sense. And hence they cannot meaningfully subscribe to the factual claims of religious statements.

Against such a critique, however, certain theologians point out that difficulties as to the meaningful understanding of the predicates applied to God arise because they are taken by the analytic philosophers literally. God is by nature mysterious and elusive and, therefore, it is difficult, rather impossible, to utter anything literal about his nature. The predicates given to him therefore have got analogical, parabolical or metaphorical meaning and they must be understood in that light. Contemporary thinkers like Lewis, Wilson, Crombie etc. all have referred to the elusive and mysterious nature of God, although simultaneously they also point out that such a nature of God must not debar us totally from an understanding of his nature. Predicates applied to God, although analogical and metaphorical in nature, still carry some cognitive sense and they must somehow be understood as such. They say something factual about God, although not literally and straightforwardly.

We will have to see all these critiques and defences in connection with the attributes of God and decide for ourselves how far these attributes are meaningfully able to maintain the factual status of religious statements.

## i. Scepticism about the Factual Nature of the Attributes

### (a) *Evil and Attributes*

Most of the criticisms against the attributes given to God have always been based on the point that facts present in the world clearly show a mutual contradiction between the metaphysical and ethical attributes of God. The empirical fact on which the contradiction of the metaphysical attributes against the ethical ones has invariably been shown is the presence of evil and suffering in this world. The arguments which have been advanced against the nature and existence of God on the basis of the existence of evil in the world we shall call Argument from Evil. Now, such arguments from evil against God are legion in the history of religious thought from very old days. Of the many ancient and modern thinkers who have presented the argument from evil, Hume[1] and J.S. Mill,[2] the two modern empiricists, have been the most resolute votaries.

Their arguments from evil are of special worth for us here because they have couched their arguments in such fairly analytic terms that they may very well be taken as precursors to the recent analytic attacks on the attributes of God from the side of the existence of evil.

The Pivot round which all the arguments from evil against the attributes revolve is the original Epicurian Dilemma, "Is God willing to prevent evil but not able? Then he is not omnipotent. Is he able but not willing? Then he is malevolent. Is he able and willing? Then whence evil?" This dilemma really presents a problem before us popularly known as the problem of evil. It is really this problem of evil which presents a very serious refutation of the attributes given to God and sometimes of his very existence. The problem of evil, says J.L. Mackie, exhibits before the theist not only that God's existence cannot be proved, but that it can actually be disproved by the very beliefs that the theist holds about God, i.e., by the very characters that are attributed by him to God.[3] Mackie presents a formulation of the problem in the form of three simple propositions:

(a)  God is omnipotent
(b)  God is wholly good
(c)  Yet evil exists.[4]

The simple point behind the problem is that, in face of the glaring fact of evil present, the world cannot be taken to be the creation of a God who is both omnipotent (all-powerful) and wholly good. He is not all-good or benevolent because in spite of his being able to do everything evils exist. And if evils exist against his kind and benevolent will, it follows that he is unable to remove them and hence he cannot be all-powerful. This is a very serious dilemma against the existence of an all-good and all-powerful God.

It can't be said that evils occur outside the knowledge of God, because he is omniscient (all-knowing) too. He is also omnipresent (present everywhere) and, therefore, evils occur in his glaring presence. Such a God, therefore, is either merciless or ineffective. The problem, thus, can never be solved, as Mackie points out, unless one of the above three propositions be removed. But then that will do away either with the very nature of God or with the real fact of evil.

However, certain solutions of the problem in justification of the nature and existence of God without sacrificing any of the above propositions have been attempted at all times by the theologians. Some of the characteristic solutions are (a) Evil is necessary as a counterpart to good, (b) Evil is necessary as a means to good, (c) Evil is due to human freewill. Now, to our mind, all these various defences of the problem of evil can somehow be subsumed under the third one. It can be seen that at the root of all the solutions, human freewill is presupposed. Evil is necessary as a counterpart to good, because without evil good will have no meaning and human beings will have nothing to choose between so as to exercise the freewill granted to them by God. Again, evil is necessary as a means to good, because unless there were evils, human beings could not have any need to work morally so that they could avoid evils and attain good. So this way also, it is for the exercise of their freewill that evil is necessary for men. Thus the freewill-defence is, at bottom, the most crucial and we will consider that.

It is sometimes said, keeping in view the human freewill, that evils are the products of man misusing the freewill given to him. God is not responsible for them. But here it is pointed out by the critic that because God is the creator of this world, he cannot be spared from the responsibility of the deeds of the wicked. If God is really good and just, he must bring the evil doers on the right track for they are his creations. And if it is not possible for God to mend such wickeds for the reason that he has granted them freewill once for all, he cannot be called all-powerful in the real sense. At least this much is beyond his capacity that he could control things if he had once made them. The situation really presents a paradox which may be called, following Mackie, the 'paradox of omnipotence'. Mackie puts the paradox in the form of a question: "Can an omnipotent being make things which he cannot subsequently control?" Or, "Can an omnipotent being make rules which then bind himself?"[5] and points out that the questions cannot be answered satisfactorily either in the affirmative or in the negative. 'If we answer "Yes", it follows that if God actually makes things which he cannot control or makes rules which bind himself, he is not omnipotent once he has made them : there are then things which he cannot do. But if we answer "No", we are immediately asserting that there are things which he cannot do, that is to say, that he is already not omnipotent.[6]

The theist or the theologian reacts against such an attack upon God's omnipotence by pointing out that God's omnipotence does not mean that God can even go against his own nature, that he can break laws quite arbitrarily. God acts like a just sovereign who, no doubt, enacts laws, but once he does so he feels himself as much bound by the laws as he wants others to be bound by them. It is for the sake of justice that he willingly imposes the laws upon himself. But according to the analyst even such a defence cannot hold, because the case of God is different from that of the sovereign. God is omnipotent which the sovereign is not. God being omnipotent should be able to find out some way so that the laws also may be maintained intact and the evil also may be removed. If this is not done, what does omnipotence mean then? And above all as Flew has elaborately argued in an essay,[7] the omnipotent God might very well have created persons who would have freedom of will but who always used their freedom to choose only the right. Flew, on the basis of a paradigm case[8] of a man freely choosing to have married a girl, argues that there would have been no contradiction in such an act of God. As he himself says: "... Omnipotence might have, could without contradiction be said to have, created people who would always as a matter of fact freely have chosen to do the right thing."[9] He really argues this by arguing the principle that freedom of will does not imply absolute indeterminism. Acting freely does not mean acting without any determination. Flew argues that even the actions which we take to have done by our own freewill (like one that of a man marrying a girl at his own free choice) are to some extent fairly predictable, because they have their source in our emotions and intentions which are, for the most, controlled by the situations in which we live. There is thus no contradiction involved in saying that an action was both free and predictable or determined. As Flew says, " ... there is no contradiction involved in saying that a particular action or choice was: *both free*, and could have foreknown, and could have been helped, and so on; and predictable, or even fore-known, and explicable in terms of caused causes."[10] Now, if it is possible, as Flew has argued, that an action can be both free and determined, then there is no contradiction in saying that God would have so given freewill to men that they would always choose the right. And hence the defence from freewill fails and the problem of evil stands.

Now, even if the analyst for the time being accepts the theistic thesis that evils are due to the wrong doing of human beings by a misuse of their freewill, it can be accepted only in case of the moral evils. What about the natural evils ? The theist may point out here that these evils may be taken as created by God, but they are for a just cause. God has made them for punishing the wickeds. But such a defence is obviously wrong and self-defeating. The natural evils do not affect only the wrong doers, but the innocents, the animals, the insects etc. too. It is a shame for a just God to punish wrongdoers and innocents indiscriminately.

Moreover, if the view that God has made natural evils to punish the wickeds is accepted, it reveals nothing but the clearly malicious and malevolent intention of the creator. Besides being omnipotent, God is also said to be all-knowing. There-fore, while creating men who are now wrong-doers, and the natural evils, he could well see what he was going to do, i.e., what would be the far-reaching consequences of his action. God's intention was clearly malicious while he created the world leaving a scope for the wicked to be punished. Everything was. within his knowledge and power and, therefore, he could well have made such a world where there were no wickeds and hence there was no need for any punishment. Moreover, it is held by many theistic religions that there is a Hell where wrong doers are sent by God. This really shows the height of God's malicious intention.[11]

Besides all these, R. Puccetti has ultilised the Argument from Evil for formulating an Ontological Disproof of the existence of God in the fashion of Findlay.[12] Like Findlay, Puccetti also first analyses the concept of God, of course, in his own way, and then argues from that, that God's non-existence is implied in the very conception of the same. Unlike Findlay, he analyses the concept of God in terms of the metaphysical and moral attributes given to him and argues that an analysis of the attributes in the light of the facts of the world (which is taken as God's creation) clearly involves God's non-existence.

Puccetti says that the concept of God is essentially the concept of an omnipotent, omniscient and perfectly good being.

Now, these properties in terms of which God is conceived cannot be understood without God being taken in relation to the world. In attributing these properties, we are not saying something 'merely about Him', but 'describe God's relation to world'. To know is always to know something, to be good is always to be good to someone.

And hence God cannot be omniscient, omnipotent and all-good in vacuum. His nature must be understood in relation to world. Now if God's nature is to be understood only in relation to the world which is taken to be his creation, Puccetti quite bluntly asks, "Is this the kind of world we should expect from an omnipotent, omniscient and perfectly good being?"[13] Certainly not. A God who is omnipotent, omniscient as well as all-good cannot be expected to have created such a world full of evil and suffering. It cannot be said in defence that God might have his own good reasons for doing so. Such a plea of defending theism is nothing but "simply leaving the question indefinitely" which is illogical.

On the basis of all these, Puccetti formulates the following argument for the non-existence of God: "(1) God must be conceived by the reflective theist as omnipotent, omniscient and perfectly good, (2) these attributes though *a priori* entailments of our God-concept, must be qualitatively symmetrical with our ordinary notions of power, knowledge and goodness, (3) the same attributes describe not only God, but His relation to everything that exists including the world of human experience, (4) there is innocent suffering in the world, (5) we would not say of a man who knowingly tolerated innocent pain which he could prevent that he is good unless there were mitigating circumstances or he had plausible reasons for doing this, (6) in the case of God, there can be no mitigating circumstances and we know of no possible reasons, therefore, (7) this world is not consistent with the concept of God and therefore (8) God does not exist."[14]

There have been several other attempts also in contemporary philosophical theology to refute theism in face of the problem of evil. There is, however, only one exception in the form of an essay by Patterson Brown.[15] Here the author quite contrary to the general trend of contemporary thinking, has ingeniously tried to reconcile theism with the existence of evils. The attempt, however, although commendable, has been seriously attacked by certain thinkers like A. Flew,[16] K. Campbell,[17] David Platt[18] etc. and in face of the criticisms, the defence hardly stands. We will, if space allows, deal with these views later on. Up to this point, we have seen that the criticisms based on the problem of Evil have tried to expose a contradiction in God's nature and sometimes even his non-existence.

### (b) *Certain Independent Analyses of Attributes*

Sometimes, apart from the problem of evil, independent attempts have been made to refute the attributes. The very notion of omnipotence, for example, it is said, is vicious apart from any particular thesis. The notion of 'unqualified omni-potence' cannot be validly maintained. God can be taken as perfectly omnipotent only if he is put beyond or outside time, because so long as he continues through time, he will be bound by causal laws. But God to be God, creating and acting through the world and the property of omnipotence to be meaningfully ascribed to him, cannot be outside time, because in that way he cannot have relationships with the world, and the notion of all-powerfulness ascribed to him will be meaningless. Thus

God's omnipotence is bound in one way or the other.. either it is bound by the causal laws or it cannot be meaningfully ascribed to him. As Mackie argues, "Quite apart from the problem of evil, the paradox of omnipotence has shown that God's omnipotence must in any case be restricted in one way or another, that unqualified omnipotence cannot be ascribed to any being that continues through time. And if God and his actions are not in time, can omnipotence, or power of any sort, be meaningfully ascribed to him ?"[19]

Similarly, the notion of 'omniscience' is self-defeating. An omniscient being is he who is all-knowing. Knowing everything means setting a limit to knowledge. Thus a being to be omniscient must be sure that there are no facts beyond what he knows. But how can the truth of this negative statement be known? How can one know that there are no facts beyond the limit he knows? Only by going beyond the limit, only by 'Peeping beyond it', but the question is, at what? Omniscience presupposes that there is nothing beyond the limit. And this shows the absurdity of the position. The knowledge of the negative proposition, that is, that there are no facts unknown, that there is nothing beyond the limit, is either absurd or impossible. But without knowing that, no being can be called omniscient. Hence the absurdity and impossibility of the notion of omniscience as attributed to God.[20]

Further troubles about God's nature and existence arise before us if we try to analyse some of the acts that are frequently associated with the name of God. God is said to have created this world. We have seen how, if God is the creator of this world, his nature is vitiated by the presence of evils in the world. Besides that, if we analyse and try to understand the notion of God's creativity itself, it seems unintelligible and creates problems for a proper intelligibility of other attributes also.

The very first question that arises with regard to the notion of creation is that in what sense the world is said to have been created by God. Is it to be understood in the sense of ordinary human creation? If so, then a serious difficulty arises which takes away the very godhood of God. Human acts of creation presuppose certain pre-existing materials out of which man creates or makes something. But if this is applied in the case of God, he is reduced simply to the role of a limited artificer, and he no longer remains infinite creator because his act of creation is limited and controlled by materials existing besides and alongside with him. To mitigate this difficulty, it is said that God has created the world *ex-nihilo*. But it is really inconceivable how one can create something out of nothing. Even if for the time being it is granted that creating the world out of nothing is possible for God because he is omnipotent, the notion of creation is not free from difficulties. If God has created the world, he has created it at a particular time. Now, the question at once arises, what was God doing before he created the world? He is all-perfect. Why did he feel the necessity of creating a world? These questions are really unanswerable. If it is said, as it is so often said, that God did not create this world out of any necessity, but he did so out of mere fun, then it seems quite peculiar that a God who is taken as kind and loving has created a world full of suffering out of mere fun. This means that he enjoys human suffering.

The doctrine of creation specially as illustrated in the Christian Genesis) implies many things more than merely certain vicious problems as to the origin of the world. In its theological sense, the doctrine entails a necessary 'ontological dependence' of the world on God, not only as to its origin, but also as to its maintenance. We are all 'creatures' of God and as his creatures we simply cannot be free, because the doctrine of creation really implies that all the power is from God, that all things and creatures are utterly dependent upon God, both for their creation and preservation.[21] In such a condition, human freedom of will really become meaningless and the defence of the problem of evil on freewill thesis falters once again here. In a creator-creature relationship, the notion of God 'rewarding' and 'punishing' also becomes meaningless. If man is utterly dependent upon God and draws his energy and inspiration from him (because as a matter of fact, the world itself does so) then punishing of men by God is not only 'morally repellent', but does not even deserve the name of punishment.[22] The theologian in thinking of man as a *creature* of an omnipotent creator and at the same time a free agent is guilty of what Flew calls in another context 'Double think'.

Similarly, there are problems as to the understanding of the meaning of the words 'loves', 'sustains' etc. also as they are applied to God. We have seen contradictions involved in God's nature when we try to understand his loving nature in face of the evil present all the world over. Now, even if that difficulty is evaded for the time being and it is acknowledged that God loves us, it is not clearly understood what God's love for us means. In what ways does he really give effect to his love? God is taken by theism as a disembodied spirit. How can a being without any body love some one? Loving someone involves the going on of certain affective, emotive processes in him who loves. Do such processes also occur in God's being? If so, how? If not, then how, after all, does he become able to express his love for us? These things are not at all clear. Similar difficulties may be raised with regard to the phrase 'sustaining' also. It is said that God sustains the world by 'acting through' it. But what this 'acting through' means? Acting always implies certain tools etc. with the help of which one works. Moreover, it [requires an embodied being. And these cannot be applicable to God, because in that case he will be a finite being. Thus, in short, the various actions-emotive, conative etc.—that are alleged of God do not make clear sense with regard to him when they are understood in the light of his complete nature.

## (c) An Estimate

We have thus seen how the various attributes given to God have been shown to be factually vacuous, self-contradictory: contradictory to each other, unintelligible, senseless etc., and thus, consequently, how they are unable to stand as meaningful descriptions of an objective reality. And we believe that, for the most part, the critiques are just in showing the factual vacuousness of the attributes of God. As far as the critique with regard to falsifiability is concerned, we have seen that the religious statements can't be falsified (at least in the sense in which scientific statements are falsified)-not only not with reference to some sense experience, but also not with reference to a supra-sensuous experience known as eschatological experience. The critique advanced from the side of evils, we think, is not less conclusive and fatal to the attributes. Of course, there have been certain attempts even in recent times to shirk from, or to meet, the difficulties raised from the problem of evil, but, we think, they have been {unable to succeed. Let us see the attempts at some length.

One such attempt can be sensed in Malcolm's contention that the attributes of God are *internal* to him, and they are to be understood in relation to themselves, and not externally in relation to something else.[23] But such a plea can hardly be maintained in view of the fact that God is the creator and sustainer of this world. His attributes must somehow bear relations with the world or, in other words, they must be understood in terms of his relationship with the world. Both Puccetti and Mackie have rightly pointed out in this connection that God's attributes really mean anything only if they describe his relationship with the world.[24] And hence, the burden of of the problem of evil can hardly be shirked on Malcolm's ground.

Another recent attempt to justify evil and to defend the nature of God even in face of it has, as we have indicated earlier, been made by Patterson Brown in his essay, 'Religious Morality'. Brown's main contention here in his own words seems to be: The hoary problem of evil rests on a misconception of religious morality.[25] What Brown wants to maintain here is that to raise the issue of evils is really to prejudge the nature of God by a prior standard of morality which is opposed ‡to the spirit of Christianity or any kind of theism. Christianity (or theism) is prior to any morality. God, he says, is 'paradigmatically good'[26] and to judge God by any ulterior standard is to deny that he is God.[27] Raising the problem of evil is nothing but judging God and hence denying that he is God. God is himself the criterion of 'goodness' and the distinction of good and evil is brought about by God's will. First there is God as the criterion of 'goodness' and then the distinction of good and evil in accordance with what he approbates and what he hates. "If God exists, then the good is denoted by what he esteems and the evil by what he damns."[28] Whence the problem of evil then? The problem of evil would have been there if the "goodness of God could be judged in terms of some ulterior ethical standard, but where is the standard before there is God? God is paradigmatically good. Christianity (and hence theism) cannot be logically posterior to any morality" [29] Evil is based on God's will and it is necessary for the Christian scheme because it is a religion of redemption from sin. Hence the existence of evils does neither disprove God, nor vitiate his nature.

This is, in short, the position of Brown. But the position is thoroughly irrational and self-defeating. Brown says that God is the criterion of goodness, he is essentially good. But how do we know that he is essentially good? Certainly by employing a prior ethical standard, and this Brown would deny as going against the real Christian sprit. Here he would perhaps say that there is no question of prior ethical standard. God is the paradigm of goodness and his "word" is to be accepted without any question as his commandment by an act of faith. But this, as Campbell remarks, "must be an invitation to a frankly irrationalist position."[30] Similarly, A. Flew remarks against such a surrender to God's arbitrary will: "It takes a very clear head—and a very strong stomach-to maintain such a position openly, consistently and without any attempt to burke its harsh consequences. "[31]

Thus evils remain a problem for the attributes given to God. The other criticisms also of the attributes of God made on independent lines rightly exposes the vagaries and absurdities involved in those characterisations.

Hence, it is clear from all the above considerations that the attributes given to God, or, in other words, the predicates given to the word 'God' in religious statements, can hardly have any sense like the predicates of ordinary factual or scientific statements. And this also implies the same thing: that religious Statements can't have the factual, descriptive or informative status as that of the ordinary factual or scientific statements.

However, this must be clearly understood that the criticisms of the attributes on the above lines are correct only if the attributes are intended as descriptions of an objective reality, i.e., only if they are used as predicates of scientific statements. The predicates may have perfect sense, if they are taken in some other light—a light other than that of taking them as genuine predicates describing some reality, as objective and factual as that of scientific facts. In other words, they have meaning not as the predicates of statements similar in nature to that of scientific ones, but as the valuational, approbative and devotional phrases used for a being whom one believes in by virtue of his intense inner conviction or faith as the creator and sustainer of the entire universe. But before coming to any such conclusion in a more solid way, let us first consider one very important plea of the theologians to save the cognitive, factual or descriptive status of the predicates given to God on the ground that they are not to be understood literally and straightforwardly, but analogically, parabolically and metaphorically.

## ii. A Defence (By an Appeal to Analogical or Metaphorical Predication)

In view of the various difficulties raised by the philosophers as to the genuine cognitive, descriptive or informative status of the predicates used in relation to God, it is so often pointed out, that religious statements are cognitive and descriptive in nature, but they are not literally or straightforwardly so. It is rather only analogically or metaphorically, that these statements convey information about a transcendent reality. God, we have seen, is a mystery and it is very difficult to say something about him quite directly, literally and univocally. Therefore, statements about God are to be interpreted and understood analogically or metaphorically. The predicates 'loving', 'wise', 'perfect', 'omnipotent', 'omnipresent', 'infinitely good' all convey information about God, but the words should not be taken applicable to God in the same straightforward way as they are applicable to human beings. However, the meaning of these words when applied to God is not also totally different from their meaning when they are applied to human beings. The ordinary use of these words has bearings, no doubt, on their meaning when they are applied to God, but they have not a literal bearing. God is not loving in the same literal sense as human beings are. However, again, it is not a fact that the ordinary use of the word 'loving' has nothing to do with its meaning when it is used in case of God. Words used for God, thus, are to be understood neither wholly univocally nor wholly equivocally. They have some resemblance in their use and meaning when they are used for God with that when they are used in case of human beings. Human analogy is thus the key to the understanding of the words used in connection with God. As the cause and creator of human beings, God possesses in some 'eminent' manner the attributes possessed by men. St. Thomas Aquinas who is famous for his doctrine of *'analogia entis'* says: "Whatever is said of God and creatures. is said according as there is some relation of the creature to God as to its principle and cause, wherein all the perfections of things pre-exist excellently. Now this mode of community is a mean between pure equivocation and simple univocation. For in analogies the idea is not, as it is in univocals, one and the same: yet it is not totally diverse as in equivocals."[32] Thus simply speaking, the idea behind the theory of analogical predication seems to be that as God is the cause and principle of the creatures, and as the effect is in essence similar to its. cause, therefore, the creatures possess the qualities or attributes. in a less perfect way, in a lesser degree, which God possesses in a more perfect, more eminent way or in a greater degree.

"Perfections are in God in a more eminent way than in creatures."[33] And hence, the incomprehensible mysterious qualities of God can be apprehended to some extent on the basis of the qualities and perfections found in men. However, the words used in relation to God are not to be understood exactly in the same sense in which they apply to human beings, nor are they to be understood as absolutely dissimilar to the latter. Human analogy gives an idea, an approximation, how to understand the meaning of the statements about God. Thus Aquinas says: "No name belongs to God in the same sense that it belongs to creatures" and "therefore, whatever is said of God and of creatures predicated equivocally"... "univocal predication is impossible between God and creatures". But again he adds: "Neither, on the other hand, are names applied to God and creatures in a purely equivocal sense as some have suggested."

Amongst the contemporary thinkers interested in the analysis of religious language, I.M. Crombie and E.L. Mascall are the two who have notably resorted to the device of analogical predication to defend the cognitive status of religious statements. Crombie's appeal to the doctrine of analogical predication is very near to that of Aquinas. However, along with the doctrine of analogical predication, he also invokes the principle of the authority of Christ side by side, and his defence of the cognitive status of religious statements made by an appeal to analogical predication depends for its validity on the authority of Christ who represents in human form a faithful image of God. The predicates like 'loves', 'wills' etc. used in relation to God describe his nature, but not literally. They are to be understood analogically. However, the analogy here is not direct and univocal. God's love is not to be understood on the strict analogy of human love. But again, the ordinary use of the word 'love' in case of human beings certainly gives us an inkling how to understand it in case of God. Through these analogies we become able to 'see in a glass darkly', but still they do not totally mislead us about the nature of God. The analogy is to be understood and interpreted in the context of a parable. Statements about

God, according to Crombie, are parables and therefore things which are said of God are said parabolically. Parables provide us with analogies-implied analogies—and these analogies somehow portray the meaning of the religious statements. If the analogies are to be taken directly and univocally, it will be difficult to realise how, when we say 'God loves us', we mean that God undergoes the same emotional and effective processes as a man undergoes in case of feeling love towards others. But when we use the analogy within the context of a parable, this difficulty is overcome, because the parables are not literally true. The point behind a parable, says Crombie, is "that you do not suppose that there is any literal resemblance between the truth which is expressed and the story which expresses it, but you do suppose that if you accept the story, not as a true literal account but as a faithful parable, you will not be misled as to the nature of the underlying reality."[34]

Thus when the analogy between an ordinary statement and a religious statement is understood within the context of a parable, the latter assumes a communication value being determined by the communication value of the former, although we do not exactly know what the divine love is like or how the words "loves' really applies to God when we say 'God loves us' "...... when we say that God loves us the communication value of the statement is determined by the communication value of a similar statement about a human subject; and that we know the statement to be right statement, but cannot know *how* it is a right statement, that is, what the divine love is like."[35] Or again, "In talking (about God) we remain within the parable, and so our statement communicates; we do not know how the parable applies, but we believe that it does apply...."[36] And "we believe that it does apply" due to our belief in the source of the parable, i.e., in Christ. We believe that Christ faithfully represents the image and ways of

God to us. In Christ's love for men, we get an authority to postulate a resemblance, an analogy, between human love and divine love.

Thus, in conclusion, what Crombie wants to convey through his doctrine of analogy is the simple fact that words used for God convey factual meanings to us and such meanings are to be interpreted and understood on an imperfect, non-literal analogy between these words and similar words used in human context. However, such analogies afford simply a dark and vague idea to us how these words are to be understood in connection with God and we cannot in any way make a definite idea how the words actually apply to God. "When we speak about God, the words we use are intended in their ordinary sense (and not in a transferred or special sense), although we do not suppose that in their ordinary interpretation they can be strictly true of him."[37]

Amongst the contemporary analysts, besides Crombie, E.L. Mascall is one important figure who makes an appeal to the theory of analogical predication to defend the factual and cognitive status of religious statements. His formulation of the doctrine contained in his book *'Existence and Analogy'* is the clearest, most important, and most widely read and approved one of all such contemporary attempts. He points out that analogies are of two kinds, and the real analogical relation between world and God cannot be understood unless we view it in terms of both the kinds of analogy—the analogy of attribution and the analogy of proportionality— taken together. The words used for God bear both these kinds of analogical relations 'interlocked' together with the words used in human context.

The analogy of attribution refers to an analogy in which one of the analogates possesses the attribute in question in an actual or, as it is technically called, in a 'formal' sense, while the other possesses the same attribute in a derivative sense. For example, in the proposition 'Man is healthy', the predicate 'healthy' is possessed by man in an actual, formal sense and it is only derivatively that the meaning of the word 'healthy' is to be understood in relation to the mountain when it is said that "the mountain is healthy. Mountain is healthy not in the sense that it possesses health, but in the sense that it produces health. The analogy of proportionality refers to an analogy where the meaning of the analogues is to be understood proportionally to the nature of the analogates to which they are applied. For example, when we say 'the dog is wise' and 'the man is wise' the meaning of the word 'wise' is to be understood in both the propositions in proportion to the nature of 'dog and man'.

Now, according to Mascall the words used for God are analogues to similar words used in ordinary empirical contexts in both these senses i.e., in the sense of the analogy of attribution as well as in the sense of the analogy of proportionality. The analogy of attribution implies that qualities of 'goodness', 'love' etc. are actually and formally possessed by men only; God possesses these attributes only in a relative or in a derivative sense, i.e., in a sense in which he is able to produce or cause these qualities in men as his creatures. Thus qualities which are found in finite objects "formally' or 'actually', exist in God only virtually. Thus 'God is good' does not mean that God possesses 'goodness' in the same way in which any ordinary man possesses this quality. It simply means that God has this quality in some such way that as creator he is able to produce this quality in others.

The analogy of proportionality, on the other hand, implies that God possesses the qualities of 'goodness', 'love' etc. in a formal way like man but each possesses the qualities in a mode that is determined by the nature of each; each does not possess them exactly in the same way. "In the strict sense, an analogy of proportionality implies that the analogue under discussion is found formally in each of the analogates but in a mode that is determined by the nature of the analogate itself."[38] Thus 'goodness' is found in man and God both but not exactly in the same way, rather 'goodness' in man is found in mode proper to the nature of men and 'goodness' in God is found "in that supreme, and by us unimaginable, mode proper to self-existent being itself".[39] Hence the formulae in which the analogy between the goodness of a man and the goodness of God is to be expressed is not, according to Mascall,

$$\text{goodness of man} = \text{goodness of God},$$

but

$$\frac{\text{goodness of man}}{\text{the essence of man}} = \frac{\text{goodness of God}}{\text{the essence of God}}$$

But then Mascall cautions here that "We must, however, beware of interpreting the equal sign too literally." The point indicated by the formulae is simply that, the goodness determined by the essence of man is appropriate to manhood while the goodness determined by the essence of God is appropriate to Godhood.

However, apart from the above strict sense of the analogy of proportionality, there is also a loose or 'spurious' sense in which this analogy is used and in that spurious use it becomes a 'metaphor'. In such a spurious sense, the analogy of proportionality implies that there is not a formal participation of the same characteristic in both the analogates, rather there is a similarity in effect they produce by virtue of possessing the analogue in question. Sometimes statements about God are used metaphorically also. For example, when it is said that 'God is angry', it implies that his relation to the punishments which he imposes is similar to that which an angry man has to the injuries which he inflicts. But no one would say that anger was to be found formally in God.[40]

## iii. An Estimate

As we have said before, the doctrine of analogical or metaphorical predication seems to have been taken recourse to by the theologians for saving the genuine cognitive nature of the predicates of religious statements when they feel like failing to do so on a literal interpretation of the same (the predicates). But let us see how far do they succeed in this attempt too. The one important point that lies behind all the above appeals made to analogical predication is that, although the predicates about God are not used in the strict analogous sense to those used about men, still the sense in which they are used in relation to man gives us an idea of the sense in which they are used in case of God. Thus all the thinkers try to save the factual, cognitive status of religious statements or invoking the doctrine of analogy, although all of them avoid the fact of univocal predication. But on examination such a plea to salvage the factual status of religious statements does not hold good. Let us see.

The very first point that can be raised against the appeal to analogical predication made in the above ways is that the appeal does not in any way make it clear in what exact sense, after all, the statements about God are to be understood. Unless one holds strong to the theory of univocal predication, which no thinker does, it seems hardly clear, for example, in what sense God loves us. And really, if it is taken in a univocal sense the trouble grows even more. Either God loses his Godhood and becomes finite or it is not clear at all what does 'love' mean in relation to a being who is disembodied. The very comparison drawn between God, who is a disembodied Spirit, and man, who is a physical being, seems out of place. Simply saying that 'love' in case of God is somehow to be understood on the analogy of human love, although not univocally, won't do. As John Hick asks, "What does 'loving' mean when it is transferred to a Being who is defined *inter alia*, as having no body, so that he cannot be thought of as performing any actions? What is disembodied love, and how can we ever ascertain that it exists?"[41] Words introduced in human context have a well-defined meaning. But if we transfer these words to a totally different context, it is absolutely unwarranted whether the words carry any clear sense. As Paul Edwards says in a relevant context, " .... it is illegitimate to use words. which have a reasonably well-defined meaning in everyday contexts to make assertions about a reality that is infinitely removed from the contexts in which these expressions were originally introduced."[42]

Crombie somehow tries to evade this difficulty by resorting to the plea of assisting the doctrine of analogy by the principle of the authority of Christ. But on such a plea the appeal to analogy really becomes superfluous and reduced virtually to an appeal to faith. If we are to believe the analogy on the authority of Christ because Christ is the faithful representative of God, do we not first appeal to faith before appealing to analogy? Does this not mean that the religious statements are analogically meaningful to only those who have a faith in the authority of Christ? And this is no appeal to analogy.

Further, if all the statements about God are to be understood analogously or metaphorically, it is really difficult to understand any one of them. For, to understand any statement on an analogy of the other; it is necessary that at least something must be known about the nature of both the analogates literally and independently. If nothing literal is known about God, i.e., if nothing is known about God in a non-analogous, non-metaphorical, independent way, then to explain one analogical or metaphorical statement we have to take recourse to another analogical statement and hence, as McPherson well realises, the circle of religion will be closed. He says in this. connection, "If we are to be able to say that statements are analogical, metaphorical, or parabolic, some at least of their terms must in the literal sense be understood by us... it does not make sense to say all religious statements have semiotic: (analogical) meaning; it would be pointless to say of some that they had semiotic meaning unless we are also prepared to say of others that they had literal meaning."[43] It is in this sense that Paul Edwards distinguishes between 'reducible' and 'irreducible' metaphors and takes religious metaphorical statements. under the second category and calls them cognitively meaningless.[44] Paul Hayner also points to this difficulty while criticising Thomas Aquinas's use of analogy.[45]

Taking the above points in view, it seems perfectly clear that Mascall's appeal to the 'analogy of proportionality', both in the strict and the spurious sense, is also not very much enlightening. If nothing literal is known about God in an independent way, is it any more useful to say that God's goodness is to the essence of God as man's goodness is to the essence of man? Or is it any good to say that "God's relation to the punishments which he imposes is similar to that which an angry man has to the injuries which he inflicts?" If we know nothing about God through any independent source, such methods do nothing to save and clarify the cognitive significance of the religious statements. The statement 'the sea is angry' is understandable, because it is, in the words of Paul Edwards, a 'reducible metaphor', but the statement 'God is angry' is not so, because it is an 'irreducible metaphor'. In other words, the statement 'the sea is angry' carries intelligible sense, because we know many things about the behaviour of the sea quite non-metaphorically or literally, but the sentence 'God is angry' is not intelligible, because we hardly know anything about God's behaviours in a literal, non-metaphorical way.

Further, any meaningful appeal to the doctrine of analogy would have meant that God possesses the attributes given to him in a far superior degree as compared to men. But seeing the nature of the attributes given to God, even this sense fails. God is said to possess the attributes in an absolute and infinite way. Now, no conceivable superior degree of power, wisdom, goodness etc. given to God can make him really omnipotent, omniscient, infinitely good etc. "By no idealization of the creaturely can we transcend the creaturely."[46] To possess the characters absolutely, infinitely and necessarily, God must possess them in a way which is different from human possession of them not only in degree but also in kind. And hence the meaningful cognitive use of analogy breaks. This also shows the irrelevance of drawing an analogy between man and God.

The most fatal point, however, against the appeal made to analogical or metaphorical predication is that such an appeal presupposes that there is a difficulty as to the meaning of the predicates of the religious statements only and the meaning of the subject 'God' is settled. But really speaking, it is the meaning of the word 'God' itself which is most problematic as to the decision of the question whether religious statements are factual or not.

Whether the word 'God' has a factual meaning or not, whether the word 'God' is applicable to a fact, is the most important point to be decided before deciding whether any thing meaningful and cognitive can be said about it. It is only when God is a reality, that the word 'God' has factual meaning, that something may be said of it analogically, metaphorically, literally or in any other way. The problem about the cognitivity of religious statements is not only a problem as to the nature of their predicates, but more importantly as to the nature of their subject. Walter Kaufmann very rightly remarks in this context, "It is a besetting fault of most discussions about the nature of God that it is simply assumed at the outset that everybody knows what "God" means, as if the issue were merely whether "He" is this or does that along with what else is already known about "Him".[47]

The above considerations clearly show the inability of any appeal to analogical or metaphorical predication to give us a clear cognitive sense of the statements about God. Besides all these, the ambiguity, superfluity and vacuity of analogical or metaphorical predication is further exposed by a practical consideration to which Flew refers when he speaks of religious statements as 'dying the death of hundred qualifications'. So long as one does not question an analogy or metaphor related to God, it seems to work somehow perfectly well to give us a meaning of religious statements. But the moment one begins questioning such analogies and metaphors, they seem to break away. Under persistent questioning, they are modified and modified, or as Flew says, 'eroded', to an extent where they become vacuous and convey no cognitive sense at all. This shows of what worth the appeal to analogical predication is in showing and defending the factual and cognitive status of religious statements.

It is clear on the above analysis that even an appeal made to analogical or metaphorical predication fails to save the descriptive nature of the predicates given to God, and hence the factual status of religious statements.

## REFERENCES

1. Hume, *'Dialogues Concerning Natural Religion'*, Parts X and VI.
2. J.S. Mill, "Nature' and 'Theism' in *Three Essays on Religion'*.
3. J.L. Mackie, 'Evil and Omnipotence', *Mind*, Vol. LXIV, 1955, p. 220.
4. *Ibid*.
5. Mackie, *ibid*., p. 210.
6. *Ibid*., p. 210.
7. A. Flew, 'Divine Omnipotence and Human Freedom', in *New Essays in Philosophical Theology*.
8. *Ibid*., p. 1-9.
9. *Ibid*., p. 152.
10. A. Flew, *ibid*., p. 151.
11. J.S. Mill, *Three Essays on Religion'*, pp. 113-114.
12. R. Puccetti, "The Concept of God' in *Philosophical Quarterly*, Vol. 14, July, 1964, pp. 237-245.
13. *Ibid*., p. 241.
14. *Ibid*., p. 244.
15. 'Religious Morality', *Mind*, April, 1963.
16. "The 'Religious Normality' of Patterson Brown", *Mind*, Oct., 1955.
17. Patterson Brown on God and Evil', *Mind*, October, 1965.
18. 'God, Goodness and a Morally Perfect World', *The Personalist,* Summer, 1965.

19. Mackie, *ibid.*, p. 212. (Here Mackie seems to have the same view as that of Puccetti, that apart from his relationship with the world God's attributes cannot be meaningfully given to him). For the view, that the very notion of omnipotence is vicious, one can also see A. Flew's views in 'Creation' included in *New Essays etc.*, Chap. IX and also his Divine Omnipotence and Human Freedom' in op. cit., where he says, " ... the whole motion of an omnipotent creator God is logically vicious", p. 165.

20. For an elaborate development of this argument one may see R. Puccetti, 'Is Omniscience, Possible ?' *Australasian Journal of Philosophy*, Vol. XLI, No. 1, May, 1963, pp. 92-93.

21. A. Flew, "Divine Omnipotence and Human Freedom' in *op. cit.*, p. 164.

22. A. Flew, "The Justification of Punishment', *Philosophy*, 1954.

23. Norman Malcolm, *op. cit.*, p. 50.

24. Our Pages 175 (for Puccetti) and 177-78 (for Mackie).

25. Patterson Brown, 'Religious Morality', *Mind*, April, 1963, p. 237.

26. *Ibid.*, p. 240.

27. *Ibid.*, p. 239.

28. *Ibid.*, p. 241.

29. *Ibid.*, p. 242.

30. K. Campbell, 'Patterson Brown on God and Evil', *Mind*, October,1965, p. 583.

31. A. Flew, "The Religious Morality of Patterson Brown", *Mind*, October, 1965, p. 579.

32. Thomas Aquinas, *'Summa Theologica'*, Part I, Article 5, quoted by Walter Kaufmann in his *'Critique of Religion and Philosophy'* (Faber & Faber, London, 1958), p. 132.
33. Walter Kaufmann, *ibid.*, p. 134.
34. 'Possibility of Theological Statements' in B. Mitchell's (ed.), *Faith and Logic*, p. 70.
35. I.M. Crombie, Theology and Falsification, in *op. cit.*, p. 128.
36. *Ibid.*, p. 127.
37. "Theology and Falsification', in *op. cit.*, p. 122.
38. From an abstract entitled 'The Doctrine of Analogy' taken from Mascall's book *'Existence & Analogy'* and included in *Philosophy of Religion'* (New York, Macmillan, 1962), edited by Abernethy & Langford, p. 372.
39. *Ibid.*
40. *Ibid.*, p. 371.
41. John Hick, Meaning and Truth in Religion' in Sydney Hook's (ed.),*'Religious Experience and Truth'*, p. 205.
42. Paul Edwards, 'Prof. Tillich's Confusions, *Mind*, Vol. 1XXIV, No. 294, April 1965, p. 198.
43. Thomas McPherson, 'Assertion & Analogy', *in op. cit.* (McPherson uses the term semiotic' here for the term 'analogical').
44. Paul Edwards, op. cit., in *Mind*, April, 1965, pp. 197ff.
45. Paul Hayner, 'Analogical Predication', *Journal of Philosophy*,September, 1958, p. 857.
46. Prof. Kemp Smith, *Is Divine Existence Credible?*, p. 14, and also quoted by John Ballie in his op. cit.
47. Walter Kaufmann, *Critique of Religion & Philosophy* (Faber & Faber, London, 1958), p. 132.

# 3
# OPPOSITION (REFUTATION) OF THE FACTUAL NATURE OF RELIGIOUS BELIEF: FALSIFIABILITY

We have seen in the preceding chapter that despite some of the deadly attempts of some of the early linguistic thinkers to strike at the very meaningfulness, and later on the factual meaningfulness of the religious statements, some very serious attempts by thinkers like A.C. Ewing, H.D. Lewis etc. were made to save the apparent meaning, i.e., factual or cognitive meaning of religious statements. But some of the linguistic thinkers were not at all inclined to save the factual meaningfulness of these statements and such thinkers devised a criterion of meaning known as falsifiability criterion, which they thought conclusively refuted any chance of these statements to claim factuality in the nature of their meaning. Although some attempts were made to safeguard the factuality of religious statements even in spite of falsifiability theory, but their attempts were finally foiled and the way was clear to give non-factual analysis of these statements. What this falsifiability criterion actually is or implies is analysed in the present chapter below and the non-factual analysis are given in the succeeding chapters.

## i. Principle of Falsifiability and the Status of Religious Belief

A very useful criterion has been developed in modern logic by Karl Popper to ascertain the factual claim of any statement. The criterion is generally known as the falsifiability criterion and was originally enunciated by Karl Popper for bringing about a clear distinction between what may be called scientific and non-scientific statements, i.e., between statements which assert and describe facts and which do not do so. As Popper himself says, "Thus the problem which I tried to solve by proposing the criterion of falsifiability was neither a problem of meaningfulness or significance, nor a problem of truth or acceptability. It was the problem of drawing a line between the statements of the empirical sciences and all other statements-whether they are of a religious or a metaphysical character....."[1] The criterion, simply stated says that, for a statement to be factual it is necessary that it does not only assert something, rather it also denies something. In other words, a statement which claims to be factual must be falsifiable, i.e., must 'forbid' something as going against it. As Popper himself says, "In so far as scientific statement speaks about a reality, it must be falsifiable; and in so far as it is not falsifiable, it does not speak about reality. And again that, the more a statement forbids, the more it says about the world of experience."[2] So, the criterion for any statement to be factual is, whether it forbids or denies anything or not. If it does not deny anything, it is not to be declared false in any situation and consequently it will be compatible with or applicable to each and every situation. Clearly such a statement cannot be said to assert any fact, because every assertion of some fact implies the denial of facts other than or incompatible with the fact asserted, and if some statement denies nothing, it also asserts nothing either. For example, if you take the statement 'The cat is on the mat' to be applicable to each and every empirical situation such that it is not to be declared false with reference to any. empirical situation, it cannot be said to assert any intelligible fact and it must be expressing, if it is meaningful at all, either some type of emotion of someone or some abnormal reaction or some such other thing.

The above criterion of the factuality of statements was. adopted into the sphere of philosophical theology by A. Flew via John Wisdom, who very competently used the criterion in an implied manner in his epoch-making essay 'Gods' (in *Logic and Language*, 1st series, ed. by A. Flew) to establish that the religious beliefs or statements were not scientific hypotheses. Wisdom. implied the criterion in his famous gardener-parable which, briefly stated, is as follows. Two gardeners return to their garden after a long gap with the apprehension that the plants must have been overpowered by that time by the undesired weeds and must have been consequently very feeble and dormant. But to their utter surprise they find some of the plants even more vigorous and beautifully grown up than what they were while they left. At this the one gardener reacts: It seems that during their absence, some gardener regularly came to garden and nourished the plants. The other, however, does not agree and retorts: who would be coming in their absence? Who could have any interest in their garden? No body actually ever came to the garden in their absence to look after and nourish the plants. Naturally, a controversy arises between the two and they try to verify in all possible ways the possibility of some gardener coming to the garden in their absence. But the results of all these verifications come to say that no gardener could ever tangibly come to the garden. But even now the first gardener goes on asserting that someone must be coming in an unseen, unheard, intangible manner, while the other asserts that no one was ever coming. Now, wherein lies the difference between the two? In point of facts? Certainly not. For, facts are all the same for both of them. The difference lies in what (or how) they 'feel' towards facts. Whenever there is a controversy involving facts, the controversy is resolved by presenting or citing facts (or instances) which go contrary to the assertion of one of the claimants. But when the situation is such that may whatever go in terms of facts, the two contestants go on asserting their respective claims without any respect or regard for the instances substantiating or refuting their claims, it means that their debate does not involve a difference regarding facts. Factual assertions are always subject to correction or refutation in face of contrary instances. And therefore, if one does not allow one's assertion to be corrected or refuted in face of any empirical situation, then surely, he is not asserting facts, although he might not be asserting a mere nonsense. Thus it seems to be the view of Wisdom as implied herein that any statement to stand the rank of a genuine factual assertion must be open to correction or refutation in face of contrary instances. If a statement is such that nothing goes contrary to it and it stands true in face of every situation, it is not a factual assertion; it may be anything else. John Hick puts the underlying principle behind Wisdom's gardener-parable in the following terms—"The underlying principle may be stated as follows: if a proposition P is to constitute an assertion, the state of the universe which satisfies P must differ, other than in the fact of including this assertion from any state of the universe that satisfies not-P."[3]

It is by drawing upon Wisdom's gardener-parable implying an important criterion that A. Flew propounds a criterion of the factual significance of assertions and then applies it to the sphere of religion so as to see whether the putative assertions about God are genuine factual assertions or not. Flew puts the criterion in a very straightforward and challenging tone in the following terms, "Suppose then that we are in doubt as to what someone who gives vent to an utterance is asserting, or, suppose that, more radically, we are sceptical as to whether he is really asserting anything at all, one way of trying to understand (or perhaps it will be to expose) his utterance is to attempt to find out what he would regard as counting against, or as being incompatible with its truth. For if the utterance is indeed an assertion, it will necessarily be equivalent to a denial of the negation of that assertion .... And if there is nothing which a putative assertion denies then there is nothing which it asserts either: and so it is not really an assertion."[4] Now applying this criterion to the sphere of religion, Flew asks us to see what it is that the assertor of the theistic statements (i.e. the religious man) would regard as counting against or as falsifying his theistic statements. If there is nothing which counts against these statements and they are compatible with each and every situation, then certainly these statements cannot be factual assertions. So, let us ask the theistic believer whether there is any empirical situation which he would regard as counting against his statements about God. Or, as Flew puts the question, let us see "just what would have to happen not merely (morally and wrongly) to tempt but also (logically and rightly) to entitle us to say 'God does not love us' or even 'God does not exist'?"[5] If the theistic believer takes nothing as counting against his statements, if he takes his statements as compatible with each and every empirical situation such that nothing makes his statements ever false, then how can he claim to make genuine factual assertions through his God-statements? J.M. Crombie puts the matter by way of clarifying Flew's position in the following words, "If they (theological statements) are compatible with any and every state-of-affairs, they cannot mark out some one state of affairs (or group of state of affairs); and if they do not mark out some one state of affairs, how can they be statements?"⁶

And the position of the theistic believer would be perhaps this : he would regard nothing as counting against or as falsifying his assertions about God. He takes God as necessarily existing and all his attributes belonging to God in a necessary manner.

J.N. Findlay, while analysing the logic of the concept of God, has rightly pointed out that any being to be called God, worth his name and position, must be such that he exists in a necessary manner and all his attributes belong to him in a necessary manner (Can God's Existence be proved?' in *New Essays* etc.). And if this is so, there is no question of the theist to regard any empirical situation as counting against God's existence or God's benevolence. He would allow no situation, for example, going against his belief that 'God loves us'. In spite of so many evils and sufferings present in the world we find that the theist goes on asserting that God is benevolent and he loves us. Thus it seems clear that nothing could falsify his statement that God loves us. He takes each and every situation to be compatible with his God-statements. He would go on asserting his statements, no matter what happens. This clearly shows that the theistic believer while uttering God-statements is not making factual statements. Flew's question "Just what would have to happen, ... to entitle us to say 'God does not love us' or even 'God does not exist'?" is to be answered simply by saying 'Nothing'. That is, no conceivable happening could ever change or refute the theist's assertion that God exists or God loves us or God is all powerful etc. It means his statements are not factual: the apparent logic of the theistic statements is not their real logic too.

But the matter does not end here. The conclusion is not final. The actual believers left apart, two strands of thought emanate from here. The one strand consists of the supporters of the apparent logic of theistic statements who somehow or other try to show that these statements are falsifiable and therefore they are factual. The other strand consists of such thinkers who take the above conclusion regarding the factual status of theistic statements as final and try to give some other kind of meaning to these statements in accordance with their use. Before taking a final decision from our own side regarding the real logic of these statements (and hence of the theistic belief), we shall have to see (assess or examine) the claims of both these strands of thought present in the realm of modern philosophical theology. For the present, however, we shall take up the first one and the second strand we will leave for the next chapter.

## ii. Falsifiability and a Defence of the Factuality of Religious Belief

### (a) *Basil Mitchell's View: A Critical Estimate*

From amongst the defences of the factual status of the theistic statements in face of Flew's falsifiability criterion, we may take up Basil Mitchell's defence first of all. Mitchell happens to be a direct participant in the famous University Discussion in which Flew as the initiator of the debate proposed his above-mentioned falsifiability criterion against the factual claims of theistic Statements. He seems to be in full agreement with Flew on the point that for any belief or statement to be factual, something must count against it. But then he complains that there is 'something odd' about Flew's conduct of the theologians' case. Flew forgets that theistic statements are the statements not of a 'detached observer' but of one who "is committed by his faith to trust in God."[7] The theistic believer or the theologian, according to Mitchell, would never deny that the fact of evil counts against God's love and benevolence.

Were he to do it, he would never have to bear the burden of the irksome problem of evil. What he would deny, however, is that the fact of evil counts *decisively* against God's love. Due to his commitment to believe in God's love, the religious believer even in spite of recognising that the fact of evil counts against God's love does not find himself ready to accept that this fact counts decisively or conclusively against that. He feels that God might have his own reasons to allow evil in the world even in spite of his benevolence. Here Mitchell relates a counter-parable against Wisdom's gardener-parable to make his point clear. A resistance-fighter after a personal encounter with a stranger and many convincing assurances from him is committed to believe that the stranger will fight from his side. In actual fighting, however, the stranger several times behaves in such a manner that it is clear that he is helping the enemy side. But still the resistance-fighter believes that he is on his side. He of course recognises on such occasions that the stranger's behaviour counts against his belief about him, but then due to his commitment he concedes that the stranger might have his own good reasons to behave like that in the interest of the resistance-fighter himself. Thus, although the resistance-fighter recognises that the stranger's behaviour falsifies his belief about him, what he does not recognise is that such behaviours decisively falsify his belief. Similarly, the theistic believer recognises that certain facts go against his belief in a loving and benevolent God, but then he does not recognise that such facts go decisively against his belief. Due to his prior commitment, he concedes that God might have his own reasons to allow such facts which go against his benevolent character.

It can be seen from the above that Mitchell tries to score his point of defending the factual status of theistic statements in face of falsifiability criterion by making a wise distinction between 'counting against' and 'decisively counting against' or else between 'falsifiable' and 'decisively (or conclusively) falsifiable'. His point seems to be that although the theistic believer allows nothing as counting decisively against his statements about God, he certainly allows certain facts as counting against them. And because he allows certain facts as counting against them, therefore his statements are to be taken as factual. But one can see it very clearly that such á distinction is hardly able to save the factual claim of theistic statements.

The distinction seems to be nothing more than to create what Duff-Forbes. rightly calls a 'verbal illusion'[8] What does it actually mean to allow something as counting against one's belief, if one holds on to his belief as firmly as ever even in spite of that something? If no amount of adverse evidence is able to shake one's belief, what is the meaning of allowing certain things as falsifying or counting against it? Mitchell maintains that no amount of pain and suffering present in the world ever finally shakes the conviction of a man that there is a benevolent God behind the world as its creator and sustainer, although he would recognise for the time being that such evils really go against or contradict his belief. But what is the real meaning of this allowance? It is just like paying a mere lip-service to Flew's falsifiability criterion. Duff-Forbes correctly holds that Mitchell's distinction. between 'counting against' and 'counting decisively against' really amounts to a distinction between 'appears to count against' and 'really counts against' and he really maintains by his distinction that although certain situations appear to count against statements about God, they really do not count against them. And this certainly is not proving the falsifiability of theistic statements in face of Flew's criterion. This is merely paying a lip-service to that criterion. W.T. Blackstone seems quite right when he concludes his survey of Mitchell's defence in the following words, "We are led to the conclusion that Mitchell pays lip-service only to the falsifiability requirement, that in the last analysis religious beliefs for him are not dissimilar to Hare's religious beliefs. In effect, although Mitchell set out to meet Flew's challenge head on, he does not meet it at all. He sidesteps, as does a slippery-half back. Unlike the side-step of a half back, however, Mitchell's side-step takes him completely off the playing field. At least, he is not playing Flew's game."[9]

## (b) *John Hick's and I.M. Crombie's View: A Critical Estimate*

Besides Mitchell, John Hick and I.M. Crombie have also tried to prove the factuality of theistic statements in face of falsifiability. Their defence of the factual status of theistic statements is rather more important and attractive. In a sense they can be said to have carried Mitchell's defence to a further extent. Mitchell pointed out that theistic statements are falsifiable, but not conclusively. If someone asks here the question, 'Why? Mitchell would perhaps answer: because they are statements of commitment'. But a more rational and convincing answer is proposed here by Hick and Crombie when they point out that theistic statements cannot be falsified conclusively by the events of this world because theism has reference not only to this world but also beyond that, and unless events beyond those of the present world are experienced, it cannot be said conclusively whether theistic belief is true or false. Theism has reference to an experience which comes in a life after death and it is only when such an experience occurs that the whole picture becomes clear. So, it is with reference to the events of this eschatological experience that it can be said finally or conclusively whether theistic statements are true or false. It is therefore not proper to seek a falsifiability of theistic statements with reference to the events or experience of this world alone. We should judge theism by putting it into its total perspective. Theism does not only say that there is a God, but also that there is a life after death in which an experience occurs which is more comprehensive than the present one. So if we have to judge the falsifiability (and hence factuality) of the statements about God, we have not to judge it by simply putting these statements into the reference of the experiences of this world alone. We will have to wait till the total picture becomes clear in our eschatological experience to decide finally whether these statements are true or false. So, because there is in principle a chance of theistic statements being falsified with reference to eschatological experience, they are to be taken as factual. If such an experience really occurs, the statements are verified to be true and if not, they are falsified. Of course, in the former case, no one will return to say that they have been verified to be true and in the latter case, the falsification will never occur as a matter of fact.

The above is a general picture of the positions taken by Hick and Crombie with regard to the falsifiability of theistic statements by eschatological experience. But the two do not put forward their views in exactly identical ways and there are certain significant differences between the two both with regard to their approach and the exact claims that they make on the basis of the possibility of an eschatological experience. It would be worthwhile, therefore, to give separate pictures also of their views and claims.

Hick repeatedly and forcefully asserts the factual status of theistic statements. But at the same time he asserts that the logic of these statements is not very easy, rather it is in an important respect both 'unique and complex'. Their factual status is not to be judged and guaranteed by ordinary means or on ordinary tests like those of the ordinary factual statements. The factual status of these statements has "the peculiar characteristic of being guaranteed by a future crux."[10] The claims of theism are not confined to the events occurring in this world alone. Theistic belief, specially the one of the type of Christian belief, is predictive of a spiritual experience which is to occur in a possible life after death. Such an experience or vision is known in Christianity as the Beatific vision or the vision of the kingdom of God. It is with reference to such experience that the truth of the theistic statements is to be verified. If, however, such an experience does not occur, these statements are falsified. But the peculiarity of the case is that although verification is actually possible, falsification is not possible as a matter of fact. For, if we have a life after death and consequently a spiritual experience of the type referred to above, we shall know that we have survived it and we shall see for ourselves the truth of the theistic statements, but if we do not have a life after death and consequently do not have any psychological experience, we shall not know that we have not it and consequently we shall not know that theistic claims have been falsified. As John Hick himself says, "The logical peculiarity of the claim is that it is open to confirmation but not to refutation. There can be conclusive evidence of it, if it is true, but there cannot be conclusive evidence against it if it can be untrue. For if we survive bodily ... we shall (presumably) know that we have survived it, but if we do not survive death, we shall not know that we have not survived it .... However, the religious doctrine is open to verification and is accordingly meaningful. Its eschatological prediction assures its status as an assertion."[11]

Hick, however, is not so much concerned with the truth of the theistic claims as with their intelligibility or meaningfulness and therefore he is anxious to establish only that it is conceivable to have a life after death and consequently an eschatological experience. And if it is intelligible to think of having such an experience, a verification of the theistic claim that 'there is a God' is also conceivable with reference to such an experience. Hick shares the view of Wisdom that theistic claims are not verifiable or falsifiable with reference to our experiences of the present world. But he is not ready to limit the verification of our theistic claims to our experience of the present world alone. According to him, theistic religions like Christianity have a belief in after-life and we can very well conceive what it would be like to have an after-life and we can also conceive what it would be like to verify that there is a God with reference to the experience that we would have in this after-life. God-statements are thus factually meaningful statements. The issue of the existence of God is a factual issue and the "choice between theism and atheism is a real and not merely empty or verbal choice."[12]

The possibility of an experience in an after-life, however, is only a necessary condition for the verification of the theistic claim that there is a God, it is not a sufficient condition. In other words, merely having some sort of experience in an afterlife would not verify that there is a God; the experience must be of as pacific nature. As Hick puts it, "Survival, simply as such would not serve to verify theism. It would not necessarily be a state of affairs which is manifestly incompatible with the non-existence of God. It might be taken just as a surprising natural fact."[13] According to Hick, our survival experience must contain the following two sorts of experiences, which if occurred in conjunction with one another would assure us beyond any rational doubt of the reality of God as conceived in the Christian faith—(1) an experience of God's purpose for ourselves as it has been disclosed in Christian revelation, and (2) an experience of communion with God as he has revealed himself in the person of Christ.

But against all these it may be pointed out first of all that although Hick claims the intelligibility of an afterlife in the form of a 'resurrection body' in a 'resurrection world', these expressions do not have very precise meaning and it is not very easily intelligible what it would be like to have a life after death in a world which is non-spatial in the ordinary sense of the word 'space' or 'spatial'. It is very much doubtful whether any precise meaning has been given or may be given to the expression 'non-physical space'

However, even if such difficulties are ignored, more important logical questions arise regarding the feasibility of the thesis of eschatological verification of the existence of God. It seems in advancing such a thesis by referring to the two above conditions of eschatological experience, Hick is in a way begging the entire question. The main question before Hick is to prove the meaningfulness (factual meaningfulness) of God-statements, such as 'there is a God', but in laying down the above conditions of the verification of these statements, Hick is really presupposing that we know or understand at least some thing about God's purpose and the image of God. Pointing towards such an anomaly in Hick's thesis of eschatological verification, Kai Nielsen remarks, "But how is Hick's claim here is verifiable even in principle, without the assumption of God—a divine Creator? We are trying to come to understand how 'There is a God' or 'God creates man' could have a factual meaning, but Hick's analysis requires us to presuppose the very thing we are trying to understand, for to speak of the 'proper destiny of human nature' or of man's final fulfilment *assumes* that man is a creature of God, a divine artifact created by God with a purpose an 'essential human nature' that can be realised. Without such an assumption, talk of man's proper destiny or final self-fulfilment is without sense. Hick is asking us to pull ourselves up by our own bootstraps, for unless we understand what it is for there to be a God who created man with a purpose we can make nothing at all of (1)"[14] (the point no. 1 as referred to above).

A similar difficulty arises with regard to the second kind of experience also. Unless we know God from beforehand, how can we recognise that the experience of communion with God in eschatological experience is really communion with God? Hick himself recognises this difficulty when he says that we do not know what it would be like to encounter directly an infinite almighty, external creator. But then he takes help of Jesus the Christ in this matter who serves as the mediator, God as revealed in Jesus the Christ gives us the hint, the clue. But here again the question is, as Nielson rightly asks, "We might decide that Jesus was a powerful man; we might verify that he did many quite amazing things; our moral insight might lead us to say he was a superlatively good and wise man; but how would this all point ambiguously or unambiguously to Jesus being the Christ, unless we independently understood what was meant by 'The Christ' or 'X's being the Christ'?"[15] Thus a similar charge of begging the question may be levelled with regard to the second condition also and Hick in effect may be charged of asking us to assume just what is in question.

Hick's begging the question becomes more evident when we come towards the end of his essay 'Theology and Verification' There he suggests that only those who had faith in God could verify the existence of God in their after-life experience; the unbelievers could not do so. But the question is, what it would mean to have faith in something about which it is still to be understood what it would be like to be that something. The question here is to decide the intelligibility, the factual meaningfulness of the belief in the existence of God with reference to eschatological experience, and therefore having prior faith in God would mean nothing. Here again therefore Hick asks us to assume what is in question. As Nielson remarks, "But what we cannot do is have faith in a proposition we do not under-stand, for in such a situation we literally cannot know what it is we are supported to have faith in... we can only have faith in something whose meaning we already understand; otherwise, we cannot possibly have any idea what we are being asked to accept on faith."[16]

Like Hick, Crombie also concedes that on ordinary levels of our experience of the present world, verification or falsification of theistic claims is not possible; it is only with reference of an eschatological experience that such claims can be verified or falsified. While we are in our present life in the present world, the whole picture is not clear. It is only when we attain a life after death that the entire picture become clear and then only we can decide whether the theistic claims are true or false. Of course, we will all be able to do that although none will return to report that he has verified. As Crombie himself says, "... since our experience is limited (at present) in the way it is, we cannot get into position to decide it.... For the Christian the operation of getting into position to decide it is called dying, and though we can all do that we cannot return to report what we find."[17] Thus what Crombie wants to imply is that although it is not possible to falsify the theistic statements into this life, we can conceive a situation in which they may be falsified. And thus because there is for them a chance in principle to be falsified, they can very well be regarded as factual. As Crombie adds after his lines just quoted, "By this test, then, religious utterances can be called statements of fact."

But in Crombie's presentation of the matter also, we can mark difficulties. First of all, we can see that Crombie seems to be talking not only of the meaningfulness of a life after death, but also of its assured truth, which is a very doubtful point.

The belief in an after-life is itself an unconfirmed hypothesis and one can understand it very clearly what can be the importance of taking to verify the truth of (or falsity) one unconfirmed hypothesis with reference to another such hypothesis. As Duff-Forbes remarks while talking of the eschatological test of theistic belief, " ... the statement that such a test can be applied to religious utterances, enabling us to say that they are factual statements is itself expressed as one of the religious utterances in question."[18]

Further, even if an eschatological experience be possible, it is still problematic to assert that the whole picture of the reality becomes clear in such an experience. Crombie asserts that while we are alive, the whole picture is not clear, but when we shall die, the entire picture will become clear and then only we can say in a conclusive manner whether our theistic claims were true or false. But the truth of such an assertion seems very much problematic. It is very much doubtful to believe that the individual, while he is alive, has only a limited capacity of experience, but when he dies he assumes the capacity of a greater vision such that he has the experience of the entire infinity of the reality.

Furthermore, obvious contradictions may sometimes be marked in Crombie's statements. It is clear from his statements that the theistic belief is just a hypothesis for the theistic believer during his life-time, and it becomes a confirmed belief only in an after life. So one can never assert the truth of any theistic statement in a categorical manner, so long as one is alive. But Crombie himself, when asked whether anything counts decisively against the belief 'God is loving' replies categorically that "No...

because it is true". The clause 'because it is true' clearly goes against the hypothetical nature of theistic belief. Duff-Forbes very characteristically remarks here, "There is little doubt that here Crombie has allowed himself the expensive luxury of a curious blunder."[19]

Finally, we can mark one more grave deficiency in the theory of eschatological verification as conceived by both Hick and Crombie. Because, according to them, the factual meaningfulness of religious belief cannot be verified unless one dies, it means that for one's whole life-time one is to take religious belief as no better than mere provisional hypothesis. But this is hardly characteristic of the belief of the religious man. He believes in the reality of God with a sense of total commitment. And thus theistic belief during one's present life-time at least represents a false and unwarranted attitude. As Mac Intyre remarks while criticising Crombie's theory, "It suggests that religious belief is a hypothesis which will be confirmed or overthrown after death. But if this is correct, in this present life religious beliefs could never be anything more than as yet unconfirmed hypothesis, warranting nothing more than a tentative and provisional adherence. But such a adherence is completely uncharacteristic of religious belief."[20]

Thus we can see that the claims for the factuality of theistic belief have not been very strongly and validly defended against the challenge posed by Flew's falsifiability criterion. The factual status of theistic belief remains in doubt and it seems that although theistic claims might somewhat otherwise prove significant, but they are surely not significant as factual claims. The factual form of the theistic belief therefore proves to be deceptive, and one has to search for the real logic of such a belief in something other than its more factual form of representation.

## (c) 'Falsifiability' and Attributes

We have seen that according to Falsifiability principle any statement to be called factual or scientific must be capable of being falsified with reference to some empirical situation. Now, one implication of the principle, as Crombie notes,[21] is that any statement claiming to be factual must be such that it delimits a definite range of application, i.e., it must be such that it is applicable to or compatible with some empirical situations (with reference to which it is verified) and it is not applicable to or not compatible with some other situations (with reference to which it is falsified). If a statement, on the other hand, delimits no definite range of application, is applicable to each and every situation, it cannot assert anything factual and it must in that case be factually vacuous. Now, God, as has been noted by Findlay, is taken not only to exist necessarily, but also to possess his attributes in such a *necessary manner* that in no case they may be conceived away. He is said to be all-comprehensive, infinitely present (omnipresent), all-knowing (omniscient) etc. How can all these attributes be applicable to God? They must be, and are, taken as compatible with each and every empirical situation. The predicate 'loving' in the statement 'God is loving', for example, is taken to be compatible with each and every situation. In face of no instance of suffering etc. the theist does allow to count anything against the statement. Hence, if God possesses his attributes in a necessary, inescapable manner so that in no conceivable circumstance they might allow anything going against them, how can they delimit any definite state-of-affair, and how can, thus, they be factually significant?

C.B. Martin has applied the principle in an elaborate way in one of his articles[22] to prove that predicates applied to God are all either factually vacuous or self-contradictory.

He takes for illustration the attribute of 'Perfect goodness' as applied to God and argues that when the theist takes God to be perfectly good, he does not simply mean that he (God) is only as a matter of fact good so that an evil nature of him can at least be conceived ; rather he takes God to be good in so necessary a manner that evil cannot even be imagined of him, i.e., nothing, no conceivable situation may be taken as counting against God's essentially good nature. Imagining unkindness of God is, according to the theist, going against God's real nature. But such a belief involves either of the two things according to Martin: (1) The belief is self-contradictory, if it claims to be factual; for, nothing can be taken to be factually applicable to something in a necessary manner. (2) Or else, it is simply tautological, factually vacuous, saying nothing factual about God, but simply defining God-concept in terms of perfect good-ness. Thus the choice is according to Martin, 'between self-contradiction and vacuity.'[23] Such an analysis of attributes is not characteristic of Martin only, but it will be acceptable to all the sceptical analysts in the field of philosophical theology like Findlay, Flew etc. And thus we may see how in a general way it has been shown by the analysis that attributes of God say nothing factually significant about him.

## REFERENCES

1. *Conjectures and Refutations*, p. 39.
2. *The Logic of Scientific Discovery*, p. 119.
3. *Faith & Knowledge*, p, 147.
4. *Theology & Falsification in New Essays*, etc., p. 108.
5. *New Essays, etc.* p. 99.
6. *Theology & Falsification, New Essays*, p. 109.

7. *Theology & Falsification in New Essays*, p. 101.
8. Theology & Falsification Again' in *The Australasian Journal of Philosophy*, Vol. 19, No. 2, Aug. 1961, p. 141.
9. *The Problem of Religious Knowledge*, p. 110.
10. *Faith and Knowledge*, p. 151.
11. *Faith & Knowledge*, p. 150.
12. "Theology & Verification' included in Basil Mitchell's *Philosophy of Religion*.
13. Ibid.
14. Eschatological Verification included in Abernethy and Langford's *Phil. of Rel.*, pp. 292-93.
15. Ibid.
16. Ibid., p. 298.
17. Theology & Falsification in *New Essays etc.*, p. 126.
18. Theology and Falsification again in *Australasian Journal of Phil.*, Aug.1961, p. 152.
19. Ibid.
20. The Logical Status of Religious Belief in *Metaphysical Beliefs*, ed. by A.C. Mac Intyre, p. 181,
21. I.M. Crombie, 'The Possibility of Theological Statements' in *Faith and Logic*, edited by B. Mitchell, pp. 44-47.
22. C.B. Martin, 'The Perfect Good' in *New Essays etc.*, pp. 212-26.
23. Ibid., p. 226.

# 4
# NON-FACTUAL ANALYSES OF THE NATURE OF RELIGIOUS BELIEF

From whatever we have seen and analysed so far it is clear that religious statements can't be factual. But then, it must be very clearly and carefully realised that this conclusion simply implies that religious statements are not factual in the same sense in which ordinary factual or scientific statements are. It is to this conclusion that our analysis so far has brought us. Nevertheless, from the conclusion that religious statements have not got the same factuality as that of scientific statements, a conclusion, very general and perhaps very natural too, has been drawn by many thinkers to the effect that religious statements are not factual in any sense, that they are something purely psychological or subjective in nature. Their obvious factual form is considered as simply deceptive and illusory, and in the light of the later Wittgensteinian slogans that (1) each kind of statement has its own logic and (2) the informal (or real) logic of a statement may be quite different from its formal (or apparent) logic, attempts have been made to seek the real, informal logic of religious statements hidden behind their apparent factual form. Now, in such a search after the real logic of religious statements (which seems to have created a competitive zeal amongst thinkers

# Non-Factual Analyses of the Nature of Religious Belief    141

for each to come up with the discovery of a new sort of logic), different thinkers have come up with different sorts of views about the nature of these statements. Some have analysed them as purely emotive, some as moral or intentional, some, again, as attitudinal and so on. In other words, some have tried to show that religious statements are simply expressive of certain emotions of religious believers: some, again, have tried to establish that they express the moral intentions of the believers and so on. In this chapter, we shall state and examine some of such views.

## i. Religious Statements as Emotive

The first attempt at giving a non-factual interpretation of religious statements is made by the logical positivists like Carnap, Ayer, Feigl etc., when they call these statements as 'emotive'. By calling them so, these thinkers want to emphasize that religious statements are purely psychological, that they have no objective root. These statements do nothing except expressing certain emotions of the religious man (and also trying to evoke similar emotions in others) habitually associated with the use of such words and expressions which constitute the so-called religious statements. Carnap compares these statements with "laughing, lyric and music"[1] which all express certain emotions.

But such an analysis of religious statements, to our mind, is not justified with reference to the believer's use of them. The term "emotion" refers to a very temporary, excited state of mind and if religious statements are taken simply as 'emotive' it is difficult to see how they are asserted so non-tentatively, absolute and non-hypothetically. Perhaps, seeing this, Carnap after first comparing religious statements with laughing, lyric and music immediately adds, "They express not so much temporary feelings as permanent emotional or volitional dispositions."[2] About volitional dispositions, we will speak later on. Let us take up here only the emotional dispositions, because it is these which are so often associated with the name of the positivists. But merely qualifying emotions or 'emotional dispositions' by the word 'permanent' won't do. Emotions are by nature fleeting. How can there be permanent emotions? To characterise what religious statements actually express in view of the fact that they are asserted with such an unflinching and unyielding sense of adherence, a word more intense and stronger than the word 'emotion' must be used.

However, in asking for the substitution of the word 'emotion' by some other word, we are not simply having a verbal quarrel with Carnap. What we want to point out is that the spirit of Carnap's analysis is not adequate to the real character of religious statements. At most, what Carnap's characterisation can show is that religious statements express certain habitual ways of reacting on the part of the believer. But does this adequately say something characteristic of the religious man's life? His religious beliefs do not express simply certain recurrent emotional tendencies on his part, rather they express his total, all-pervasive way of responding. Religious responses seem to involve the whole man and they have their impression on the whole of man's life. His ways of responding can't be taken as simply certain emotional reactions. The word 'reaction' is too shallow to express the intensity of religious man's response.

Moreover, even if religious statements be taken as expressions of certain emotions, or emotional dispositions, it is to be seen that even emotions are not purely subjective. They have some objective anchorage. Emotions are always in relation to some objective situation. The positivists seem to say that religious statements express certain emotions associated with or aroused by certain words like 'God', 'Soul' etc. But these words also cannot be able to arouse specific emotions within the religious man unless at least for the believer they refer to certain objective situations. And specially when one talks of permanent emotional dispositions, he must realise that such emotional dispositions must have their base in certain very crucial situations facing at least the believer within whom such emotions are aroused. Emotions to be permanent must be something more than mere emotions. They must be backed up and sustained by certain situations which may seem to the believer very lively and objective. And again, there is not only one or two, but a whole community of believers all of whom express similar emotions. How can then religious responses. be merely subjective emotions?

Again, if through religious statements, the religious men simply express their emotions, how do the religious statements. take perfectly objective or factual forms? Where-from do they derive their objective force? Why are they put in direct subject-predicate form of sentences? If such statements were expressing mere emotions, then they might have been expressed by merely employing certain interjections. Religious statements do not asset objective facts, it is true. But again they can't be taken as purely emotive. Even if through his statements, the religious man were expressing his unique psychological state of mind, he must be doing so in face of some situation which looks perfectly objective to him; otherwise he would not have uttered indicative sentences. This shows that religious statements are something more than merely emotive.

## ii. Religious Statements as Statements of 'Confession', 'Conversion', 'A Free Decision Made in Faith and Love'

Such is the view of MacIntyre as propounded in his long and important essay 'The Logical Status of Religious Belief'. A portion of the essay MacIntyre devotes to show the factual vacuousness of the religious statements with the same spirit and the same technique as employed by A. Flew. Because no empirical circumstance will be allowed as counting against the religious statements, therefore, according to Macintyre, they cannot be taken as factual. But unlike Flew, he does not stop here. He acknowledges that religious statements have their own logic. And that logic is the logic of confession, of worship, of total commitment; of unconditioned adherence. That is, religious statements express or signify the believer's sense of total commitment to something which (or whom) he takes to be his God. They are statements of 'trust', of unquestioning confession. They signify some one's unconditional conversion to some faith. Tentative adherence and expectation of facts supporting or going against his belief is absolutely uncharacteristic of the religious believer. His believing in God is a 'decision' taken by him once for all by virtue of his love for and trust in some one whom he has accepted as his God.

Now, such confessions or conversions, according to MacIntyre, have no objective roots. They are simply subjective. "To believe in God resembles not so much believing that something is the case as being engrossed by a passion."[3] There is thus no objective or rational justification for holding religious beliefs. They are absolutely irrational, based on subjective considerations. The decision is taken by the believer only out of the subjective passion or love that he feels for someone. ".... to accept religious belief is a matter not of argument, but of conversion ... the transition is not in objective considerations at all, but in person who comes to believe."[4] The only justification that one can find for the religious belief is in Authority. The religious believer accepts his beliefs on the authority of some prophet or messiah, or the scriptures, tradition etc. There can be no other source of justification for his belief. "Religion is justified only by referring to a religious acceptance of authority."[5] Thus religious statements, according to MacIntyre, are nothing but statements of 'total commitment' based on purely subjective considerations and having for their only justification an authority.

The above is a very brief outline of MacIntyre's views on religious belief. MacIntyre really does a great service to religion by pointing out that religious statements are not factual or tentative hypotheses; they are statements of such an absolute and total adherence that taking them in any way as factual hypotheses at all is "to falsify both the kind of belief they are and the way in which they are characteristically held."[7]

But let us now see some further implications of his view. In analysing religious statements as statements which express the believer's sense of total commitment, MacIntyre's claim is "only to describe how religious language is in fact used."[8] But to this we have to point out that in describing religious statements, he has taken only a partial view of their nature. If one is to describe religious statements as they are in fact used, he must see that these statements are in fact used in two such ways. which seem contradictory to one another—(1) They are used as statements of total commitment. (2) They are used as factual statements with full factual force. MacIntyre picks up the first as it stands and on the second he begins to advance logical considerations. Where does his analysis then remain simply descriptive? In one aspect it becomes prescriptive. By prescribing on the one feature of religious statements, he claims to be descriptive of the other. If he claims to describe religious. statements as they are in fact used, he has no right to take these statements as expressions of 'being engrossed in a passion'. On his analysis, God becomes a subjective fiction of the believer's mind or something given by an authority, but does the religious believer take his God ever as merely something subjective? Where does the analysis then remain simply descriptive?

As a matter of fact, in our view, the mere description of religious language cannot give one its real logic. The real logic can be found by looking into the ways in which the believer is actually concerned while uttering these statements. What, after all, is actually involved in the religious situation that makes the believer assert the religious statements with two seemingly contradictory spirits, viz., asserting the religious statements as. factual statements and still not allowing anything to count. against them? It is in a satisfactory answer to this question that the proper analysis of the logic of religious statements lies.

Further, MacIntyre takes religion as a matter of total commitment and at the same time purely subjective, having no rational or objective justification for it. There seems to be an obvious contradiction in these two attitudes. How can an unquestioning and absolute adherence as MacIntyre takes characteristic of religious beliefs can come about without somehow being in face of a very crucial and objective situation? There may not and, perhaps, cannot be rational grounds in the sense of logical arguments for total commitment, but there must be some objective situation, a situation which may or may not be objective in the public sense, but which must have some objective force and crucial significance for the believer. The logic of total commitment, in our view, demands that the commitment may be non-rational, but it cannot be irrational. It can't take place in complete absence of any reason.

However, MacIntyre, or someone from his side, may press here that religious commitment may be the commitment of a neurotic or a hysteric who responds without any objective situation as if there were one and is immune from any reasoning whatsoever. But such a total commitment which is absolutely unchangeable and impervious to any reasoning or situation does not seem adequately characteristic of the religious commitment. If the total commitment were completely absolute and entire, how could conversions, from one belief to another, or sometimes even from belief to unbelief, be possible? (However, the commitment is total in the sense that so long as one stays under one particular faith, he observes its beliefs with a sense of unreserved, unconditional assent). This shows that religious convictions or commitments are not of the neurotic type. They are sane in nature. And any sane commitment, however deep-rooted it may be, has got the chances to be forsaken in face of some overwhelmingly contrary instances. As a matter of fact, no commitment, no 'blik' is wholly irrational. It depends upon certain real circumstances and has to be somehow justified on rational grounds. Reason cannot produce total commitments, but it can certainly justify them. It is unfortunate that Hare's blik-theory has been compared to an insane lunatic's irrational sense. Even bliks are to be justified on certain evidences, rational or empirical. The theistic proofs, perhaps, serve this purpose. "Unconditional belief does not mean being immune from all logical refutations.... The unconditional adherence which the Christian owes to God requires that he should resist temptation to deny Him, not that he should reject considerations which ought to convince him that he is mistaken."[9]

Besides all these, we find MacIntyre characterising religious beliefs as 'free decision made in faith and love'. The expression *'free decision'* is to be marked here. How can religious beliefs, if they are *decisions*, be wholly irrational and insane having no rational or objective justification? Can there be any decision without any rational or objective consideration? As Prof. Root remarks in this context, "We should scarcely use the term 'decision' at all if we were acting in the complete absence of any reason."[10] The notion of freely accepting a belief and still lacking in any rational grounds for that, has, according to Root, an 'echo of popular existentialism' in it, because here we are condemned to be free, but all our choices are then absurd.

## iii. Religious Statements as Volitional or Moral

Some thinkers, again, have detected a purely volitional or moral meaning in religious statements and accordingly they have advanced an intentional or moral analysis of them. One very characteristic example of such an analysis can be seen in Prof. Braithwaite's view expressed in his famous Eddington Memorial lectures ' *An Empiricist's View of the Nature of Religious Belief.* The essence of Prof. Braithwaite's view here is that religion is essentially an ethical or moral outlook, and therefore religious statements are nothing but the expressions of the believer's will or intention to act in a particular way or to lead a specific way of life. And it is this function of expressing the believer's intention to lead a specific way of life that that gives religious statements their meaning. As Braithwaite says, ".....the meaning of a religious assertion is given by its use in expressing the assertor's intention to follow a specified policy of behaviour ... it is the intention to behave which constitutes what is known as religious conviction."[11] The statements of any particular religion, therefore, express its followers' intention to lead a particular way of life. The statements of Christian religion, for example, express the intention of the Christians to lead what Braithwaite calls an 'agapeistic way of life', i.e., a life based on the ideal of each one's love for his neighbour. What is over and above these moral policies in a particular religion is what Braithwaite calls 'stories' or 'parables' or 'myths' etc. By a 'story' Braithwaite means "A proposition or set of propositions which are straightforwardly empirical propositions capable of empirical test and which are thought of by the religious man in connection with his resolution to follow the way of life advocated by his religion."[12] One important point to note with regard to these stories is that, according to Braithwaite, it is not essential that these stories are true. Even this is not necessary that the followers of a religion should believe the stories to be true. "What is necessary is that the story should be entertained in thought i.e., that the statements of the story should be understood as having a meaning."[13] These stories are valuable in as much as they are psychologically helpful in 'bolstering up' the believer's intention to adopt a particular way of life. These stories, however, are not central to any religion. What is central is the moral policy that it involves or implies. The stories simply back up or support the moral intentions or policies. However, these stories are important in as much as they distinguish one religion from another. It is possible that two religions advocate the same moral policy (as Buddhism & Christianity), but what distinguishes the one from the other is the set of particular stories with which the one is associated and the other is not (the other is associated with a different set of stories). Moreover, it is these stories with which religious statements are essentially associated that distinguish them from purely moral statements.

The above is a brief sketch of Prof. Braithwaite's views on the nature of religious beliefs or statements. More or less, a similar view has been advocated by R. W. Hepburn in his book *Christianity and Paradox*, specially in chapter XI. According to Hepburn, like Braithwaite, religion is a way of life associated with a 'parable'. Religion has primarily a moral function. Different religions are nothing but the expression of different ways of life or codes of moral principles intended to be taken up by their followers. This purely moral function is backed up in religion by certain parables. These parables in Hepburn are, more or less, the same as Braithwaite's 'stories' and their job is. As Hepburn says, "Mainly that of backing up a bare moral rule with an imaginatively vivid instance of its being practised or neglected."[14] Again, just like Braithwaite, Hepburn also believes that it is not essential for these parables to be true. They can do their jobs of backing up the moral rules even if they are purely fictitious. The only thing necessary is that the religious people think of them as being associated with their moral intentions. As Hepburn says, "It is not of paramount importance whether or not the story or parable is historically true. It can do its job equally well if fictitious; sometimes better."[15] Further, just like Braithwaite, Hepburn also holds. that of the two, the moral pattern of behaviour and the parable, it is the former which is central and the latter has only a subsidiary function. As he clearly says in this connection, "The moral pattern of life is the fundamental thing: the story its vehicle."[16]

Now, if we consider religious language as a whole, it is undoubtedly moral to a great extent. Not only it is that a large number of sentences comprising religious language are moral sentences, but also that morality has got a very essential and intimate relationship with religion. As Hare-very rightly says, "... all religions have what may be called a moral aspect. By this I mean, not merely that the adherents. of a particular religion have in fact usually adhered to a particular set of moral principles, but that the moral principles. are linked in some intimate way with the religious belief."[17] But from this it does not follow that moral principles constitute the whole of religion. Hare is much honest when he frankly acknowledges that "the moral judgments... arise out of religious belief; they do not constitute it."[18]

And specially, it does not seem at all clear in the case of straightforward indicative religious statements like God is benevolent, God is infinite, God is the creator etc.) how they can be nothing but purely moral in character. It is not at all clear, if religious statements are seen in relation to their assertors, as to how, while uttering these straightforward statements of subject-predicate form, they are expressing their intentions to act in a particular way. In this light, Braithwaite's and Hepburn's analyses of religious statements seem to be purely prescriptive having no relationship with their ordinary usage. It is clear from our previous analysis that ordinary usage of religious statements in the strict factual sense is not correct, but it will be something too doubtful to conclude therefrom that the apparent logic of these statements has absolutely nothing to do with their real logic. Braithwaite-Hepburn thesis seems not so much analysing the nature of religious Statements as prescribing something about their nature: perhaps, as to how they *should be taken* in the light of an empirical outlook which has been the characteristic of the Western philosophy since the end of the first world war. The very title of Braithwaite's lecture amply shows that he is not to give a neutral analysis of religious statements, rather he is to present 'an *empiricist's* view of the nature of religious belief'. This is all the more clear from his statement that he makes towards the beginning of this lecture, "Since I wish to continue to employ verification in the restricted sense of ascertaining truth-value, I shall take the principle of meaning in this new form (use-principle as he calls it) in which the word 'verification' has disappeared. But in removing this term from the statement of the principle, there is no desertion from the spirit of empiricism. The older verificational principle is subsumed under the new use-principle : the use of an empirical statement derives from the fact that the statement is empirically verifiable ...."[19] The statement clearly shows that while analysing religious statements Braithwaite's mind is haunted, somehow or other, by the same old ghost of verifiability and he is anxious to show the meaningfulness of religious statements in the overt actions. of religious persons. Ronald Hepburn is also suffering from the empiricist bias while presenting his own analysis. But Hepburn has, unlike Braithwaite, fewer pretentions. He frankly admits that his analysis does not admit of Christian religion (or of any theism of that kind), but still he takes his analysis as *valuable* (and not true) in as much as it brings a valuable reconciliation between empiricism and religion. As Hepburn himself says after admitting that his analysis is not true to traditional Christianity, "If I conclude, then, that an account of religion in terms of a moral way of life backed up by parable fails as a description of Christianity, I do not want to go on and say that we can therefore count if of no value. For I see in it one way of answering some of the religiously minded sceptic's worries; and of answering them most satisfactorily ...."[20] All these clearly show that the Braithwaite-Hepburn thesis is purely prescriptive in character and it fails absolutely to account for the believer's use of the religious statements with full factual or cognitive force.

Moreover, if religious statements express merely the *intention* of the believer to follow a specific policy of behaviour, the fact as to why religious man asserts them so tenaciously remains unexplained. Mere intentions to act in a particular way may change very easily if one has to face adverse consequences by acting that way. On Braithwaite's analysis, the statement 'God is benevolent or loving', for example, may be interpreted to express the believer's intention to lead what he calls an agapeistic way of life, but it must be realised that mere intention (and hence such a belief) to act in this particular way would have been changed in face of obvious evil consequences faced by a man performing good actions. This clearly shows that religious statements express something deeper, something more intense, than mere intentions to act in a particular way. Or again, they do not express bare intention, but intentions surcharged with certain deep feelings and initiated and backed up by certain such cognitions which somehow involve the whole man. Mathew Arnold defined religion not simply as morality but as 'morality touched by emotion'; and Kant thought it essential for morality to be hallowed by some faith in God. Intentions to act always in a confirmed and specific way must be something more than mere intentions. Hepburn seems more alive to this aspect of religious statements when he says that such statements express a sense of *"commitment"*[21] of the believer to a pattern of ethical behaviour and that the pattern of behaviour is concerned not only with any fraction of the believer's life but for every aspect of it. The word 'commitment' involves much more than mere intention or will. It includes the whole man in his affective, cognitive and conative aspects.

A still further moral analysis of religious statements has been given by T.R. Miles in his book *'Religion and Scientific Outlook'* in his own characteristic way. Here Miles seems keenly averse to taking religious statements as factual statements. He very strongly refutes the notion of what he calls 'absolute existence'[22]. By absolute existence he means the existence of a real entity over and above the ordinary empirical objects of the world. Such an existence he also calls 'para-physical' or 'para-empirical' and points out that the notion of such an existence is meaningless. The statements of theism, according to him, taken literally are either meaningless or false. They must, therefore, be taken parabolically. Theistic statements are parabolic statements. The points behind a parable according to Miles are :

a. The question of their literal truth and falsity is unimportant.

b. Parables contain, for the most part, assertions that are empirical and that can be verified and falsified.

c. Parables convey messages or morals.[23]

Religious statements are thus essentially moral in character. They convey moral messages. Their literal form is misleading. Having theistic beliefs or asserting religious statements, then, means nothing but accepting certain parables or morals. Believing in God means accepting the theistic parable. And accepting the theistic parable means giving assent to, or expressing a total allegiance to, a specific way of life. Miles himself says, "Believing in God means accepting the theistic parable."[24] And again, "Accepting the theistic parable involves conversion and a change of outlook."[25] Religious statements, thus, according to Miles, are essentially moral in character and accepting them or asserting them means expressing one's allegiance to a specific way of life.

This, in brief, is the view of Miles about the nature of religious statements and we can see that in presenting such a view he has an essential affinity with Braithwaite and Hepburn. In giving religious statements a meaning only if they are taken parabolically or morally, Miles is presenting the same prescriptive analysis of religious statements as that of Braithwaite and Hepburn. There are parables, no doubt, in religious language which carry implicit morals, but to take even the straightforward indicative sentences (like God exists, God is so and so) as parabolic seems something strange and essentially prescriptive. Miles has no other explanation for the ordinary man's use of these religious statements as factual statements except that they are meaningless or false. Here he is guided more or less by the same spirit as that of the positivists. He sums up his characterisation of religious beliefs as 'Silence qualified by parables'. This simply implies that religious statements taken as they apparently stand are either false or meaningless and therefore it is better to remain silent about them. "The questions whether there is such an entity (God as an extra entity') and whether the theistic parable is objectively true can be met only by the 'way of silence."[26] Miles' silence about the religious statements, as he himself tries to clarify, is not the mystic's silence, but the silence of one who takes these statements as absurd.[27] However, if these statements are taken as parables, they imply sense and one can talk about them.

To all these, we have simply to point out that it is correct, no doubt, that theistic statements are not to be taken literally as genuine factual statements, because being so taken they raise issues which are not meaningfully soluble. But this is not the same thing as saying that the theistic believer has no reasonableness of his own to use religious statements as factual. Wisdom is very correct when he points out that although the issue between theism and atheism is not a factual one. Still from this, "We must not forthwith assume that there is no right and wrong about it, no rationality or irrationality, no procedure which tends to settle it nor even that this procedure is in no sense, a discovery of new facts."[28] A philosophical analysis of religious statements, as we have said earlier, must not only prescribe. It must also analyse the real implications behind the current usages of them. The prescriptive element must be derived out of the descriptive one, and not that the structure of the former is to be erected on a complete annihilation of the latter. In giving an analysis of the religious statements in the above way, Miles, it seems to us, points out not what religious statements mean, but what they *ought* to mean.

## iv. Religious Statements as Evocative of All-pervasive Dispositions—Mental, Physical and Emotional

One such analysis of religious statements can be seen to have been carried out by Kennick in his article 'The Language of Religion'. Kennick seems to be of the view here that religious statements "articulate, arouse, sustain and modify" certain all-pervasive dispositions to respond to objects, events and persons in certain specific ways. That is, these statements arouse, sustain (etc.) certain dispositions which make one act in relation to persons, things and events always in some specific ways. Such responses or actions may be physical or they may even be only mental, i.e., only in terms of thinking and feeling in certain specific ways. The entire thing can be best expressed in Kennick's own unambiguous language, "The distinctive purpose of religious discourse is to articulate, arouse, sustain and modify attitudes."[29] By attitudes is meant "dispositions or predispositions to respond to objects, events and persons in certain limited ways, whether the responses be overt actions, or feelings, or ways of thinking."[30] And again, "The attitudes that define and constitute it (religion) tend to embrace and permeate the whole mind and the whole sensibility of the religious man or group."[31]

Another such analysis with somewhat a greater zeal and detailed clarifications has been carried out by Paul Schmidt in his book *Religious Knowledge*. Schmidt's view regarding the nature of religious statements seems to be very near to that of Kennick. Although he openly acknowledges the allegiance of his views to those of Braithwaite[32] and Ian Ramsey[33] and only pays a passing tribute to Prof. Kennick in the preface of his book, it seems to us that he has the greatest affinity in his views with Kennick himself. He has, of course, gone much farther than Kennick in as much as he has tried to understand the nature of religious statements with deeper insight and unparalleled clarity and has also marked broader horizons of implications of these statements, but in essence, he fully shares the views of Prof. Kennick. This will be perfectly clear from the brief picture that we draw here of Schmidt's views.

According to Schmidt, just as according to Kennick, "The primary purpose of religious language is to produce certain attitudes in oneself and in others."[34] Of course, Schmidt drops here certain words like 'articulate', 'sustain' and 'modify' as used by Kennick and concentrates upon the evocative role of religious statements.

An attitude, again, according to Schmidt, is "a disposition of a person to behave (think or act) in a particular way."[35] And a disposition is "a readiness or propensity or tendency to behave."[36] The disposition need not actually occur, i.e., need not be expressed in terms of actual physical behaviour. It may even be emotional or mental.

Again, like Kennick, Schmidt also holds that attitudes Which religious statements arouse concern not only a part of one's life or an aspect of his being, but with the whole of it. They permeate the entire being of the religious man and persevere all through his life. Such attitudes, in other words, are all-pervasive. Again, not any pervasive attitude is to be taken as religious according to Schmidt, but only those which are "concerned with human relations, with relations to other parts of nature and with an outlook regarding the whole of nature and life."[37] And here, perhaps, Schmidt marks an advancement upon Kennick's view in as much as he, unlike the latter, specifies what kinds of attitudes are to be taken as religious.

Summing up the whole of Schmidt's above views, we can say that religious statements arouse in oneself and in others certain all-pervasive dispositions to act —whether in physical, mental or emotional terms—in certain specific ways in relation to nature, man and life in general.

The essence of the above view as preached by Kennick and Schmidt seems to be that religious statements arouse all- pervasive attitudes to lead a specific way of life in all its physical, mental and emotional aspects. Now, it is to be marked that these thinkers use the term 'arouse' or 'induce' or 'evoke-invoke' and not 'express'. In other words, they do not say that religious statements express attitudes but that they *arouse* or *induce* attitudes. This shows that they do not analyse religious statements from the side of the believer, i.e., from the point what the believer *does* (for himself) when he uses or utters religious statements, but from the side of other persons who would describe the believer, i.e., from the point what the believer *wants or intends to do* when he uses the statements. Such an analysis of, or talk about, religious statements Schmidt calls 'outside talk', i.e., a talk as to 'how another person would describe the believer'[38] and he argues for preferring such a talk because it is saved from 'the notorious difficulties that introspection leads to in psychology'. An 'inside talk', i.e., a talk from the side of the believer, would involve the introspective reports of the believer and so he has avoided such a talk. But we, on our part, do not approve of such a plea in the analysis of religious statements. An analysis of religious Statements by keeping them apart from mind of the believer, i.e., a purely extrospective analysis of them, would lead to nothing but artificial results. Any proper analysis of these statements must be from the side of those who use them, i.e., from the side of the believers. A purely outside talk about religious statements will make them nothing but certain artificial tools for evoking arbitrary attitudes. *Evocation* of specific, and not arbitrary, attitudes is essentially connected with the *expression* of certain attitudes. Through religious statements, the believer, no doubt, wants to arouse certain specific attitudes in himself and in others, but this he can do only if his statements contain the potential of the attitudes he wants to evoke. That is, he first *expresses* certain specific attitudes through the religious statements and then uses them with the purpose of arousing similar attitude in himself on subsequent occasions and also in others. Unless one's statements first contain or express certain attitudes, how can they be meaningfully used to evoke similar attitudes in oneself and in others? What will the 'purpose of the evocation of certain specific attitude' mean then? Thus it is not only that religious statements evoke certain attitudes, but they also express such attitudes of the believer. And it is not only on the basis of introspection that one can say so, but also on a sincere objective study of a vast number of religious statements as used by the believers. Although while specifically analysing the meaning of religious statements Schmidt carefully uses the term induce' or 'evoke-invoke' and also argues for the justification of these uses, at other places he uses the term 'express' also. As for example, on page 111 of his above-mentioned book he clearly says, "The purpose of religious statements is to express attitudes that lead to a way of life?" Again, while analysing the meaning of specific. religious statements on page 92, he invariably uses the word 'express', i.e., he analyses them as expressing attitudes.

Now, if Schmidt gives up his bias for what he calls 'outside talk' and is prepared to admit an 'inside talk' about religious statements, his (and also Kennick's) analysis marks a definite advancement upon positivist's emotive and Braithwaite's moral or intentional analysis. According to him religious statements neither express mere emotions nor simple intention, but 'attitudes'—pervasive attitudes, and such attitudes include within themselves all the emotional, physical and mental dispositions of man. Hence, when one utters religious statements, he expresses not only his emotion nor his mere intention, but his entire personal disposition in all its aspects; he, in a way, expresses his total adherence to a specific way of life. It is therefore easy to see how he asserts the statements so non-tentatively and non-hypothetically.

But in another respect, again, these analyses are like those of Braithwaite and Hepburn themselves. When Kennick and Schmidt say that religious statements express pervasive attitudes to lead a way of life, it is different from Braithwaite's saying that religious statements express intentions to lead a way of life in the only fact that whereas Braithwaite takes religious statements as expressions of *intention*, Schmidt takes them as expressions of *attitude*, and consequently, whereas by 'way of life' the former means overt moral behaviour, the latter means by it also the emotional and mental dispositions to act. But from this difference the essential nature of the analysis does not change. Schmidt's analysis is as much prescriptive in nature as that of Braithwaite. If religious statements simply express certain specific attitudes (i.e., dispositions to act) and have got no other implication besides it, then why are they used as factual statements? Schmidt does not analyse believer's use of the religious statements, but his own way of thinking about them. He points out that "To say that God is omniscient is to express the attitude of continuous search for the solution of problems and of action that awards a high place to knowledge."[39] is Again, "To say that God is omnipotent is to express the attitudes of being subject to higher powers, of admiration for the grandeur, vastness and intricacy of nature ......"[40] And, "To say that God is benevolent is to express the attitude of being kind to others......"[41] But are these analyses of religious statements in consonance with their use by religious believers? Are these not arbitrary prescriptions and superimpositions of a master mind? If the statement 'God is omniscient' is used for evoking attitude of continuous search for the solution of problems and acquiring of knowledge, why this indicative form? Why not is it used as clear precept—'Search for the solution of the problem continuously up to infinity' or 'It is advisable or desirable to search for solutions continuously.' Similarly, if the statement 'God is benevolent' is used to evoke such attitudes as being kind to others, why not is it used as the simple saying 'Be kind to others', or 'It is good to be kind to others'? Why in the form of descriptive statements? What is the meaning of 'God' in all these sentences? Schmidt says, "Theological statements. express attitudes connected with God."[42] But what is this "God" for? What does it mean? Schmidt perhaps does not make it clear.

In short, what we want to point out is that it is, no doubt, correct to say that religious statements express an all-pervasive attitude towards world and life in general, but if such attitudes are interpreted as merely certain dispositions or readiness for actions so that religious statements become merely the expressions of a readiness on the part of the believer to have a specific pattern of life, then here we commit the fallacy of simply ignoring the point behind the factual force with which the religious statements are asserted. As a matter of fact, an all-pervasive disposition or an all-pervasive readiness to lead a specific way of life, which is characteristic of the religious. believer according to Schmidt, cannot be simply subjective and arbitrary. Such a readiness presupposes a crucial *decision* on the part of the believer and in having that crucial decision once for all for the entire life in all its aspects, something very significant would have been at stake. Reason cannot bring one to such decisions, because it is unable to give one a total, comprehensive picture of world and life as a whole. Unless one finds some novel and at the same time overwhelming significance in world and life (which the others perhaps do not): and unless the new significance *impresses* him in a sound and objective way, he can't be made to express such an all-pervasive readiness to lead a special pattern of life. Thus before assuming a pervasive readiness for a specific pattern of behaviour concerned with general human relationships and with world and life in general, one must have been impressed in a specific way by world and life as a whole. It is such a vision of a new dimension in the world and life as a whole which gives the religious statements a full objective force and makes them at the same time potentials for an all-pervasive pattern of specific behaviour.

The whole thing is taken by Schmidt in a way he takes it perhaps due to his conception about religion that it is literally "a way of life"[43]. It is due to this conception of religion that he interprets religious statements in purely dispositional terms. Religion is undoubtedly a way of life, but a way of life, specially when it is constant and unsurrendering in all circumstances, must be based on certain convictions, certain persuasions about life and world in general. A way of life or, in other words, a 'pervasive pattern of behaviour' must be based on a strong conviction towards world and life. Convictions, says Zuurdeeg, are 'strong persuasions' which generate a 'certitude which is a sufficient ground for action'[44]. Religious statements express such strong convictions which in consequence *lead* to a pervasive way of life and not that they directly express a readiness or a disposition to *lead* a pervasive way of life. Religion, to our mind, is first a specific kind of conviction in regard to world and life as a whole and then a way of life, the former inevitably leading to the latter.

Now, convictions, we have seen, are strong persuasions. Thus, being convinced in relation to world and life in general, so that a specific and pervasive pattern of behaviour may follow, one must be 'strongly persuaded' by world and life in general in a specific way. Now, what does this 'being strongly persuaded' in a specific way in relation to world and life mean and imply? Being strongly persuaded implies, as Zuurdeeg says, being 'over-powered', 'overwhelmed', 'fascinated' or 'convicted' by some presence-objective presence in the world-and-life situation as a whole. The persuaded man somehow really detects a new dimension in the world and life which others miss and it is in face of the vision of that new dimension that he is so strongly persuaded in regard to world and life as a whole in a specific way. Every convictional situation, says Zuurdeeg, implies at least three important things—a convictor, a convictus and a decision. The convictor is the crucial objective presence which overpowers. The convictus is the man who is overpowered. And the decision is the 'assent' that the man gives to the overpowering presence. Such a decision, says Zuurdeeg, "is a dedication of the person to the convictor because something of overwhelming importance is at stake. "[45] It is really in such a convictional situation that the man takes a crucial decision to dedicate his life to a particular cause and consequently wears a specific and pervasive pattern of behaviour. The decision involves a commitment on the part of the man and it brings a total change in him. In the religious convictional situation, the convictor is always the God, and as. all convictors in any convictional situation are perfectly real and objective at least for the man who is in the convictional situation as well as for all those who share his conviction, God also as the convictor of the religious situation is perfectly real for the religious community which shares the same conviction.

Hence, religious statements before being expressions of a pervasive pattern of behaviour in relation to world and life, are expressions of some strong conviction in regard to them, and in such a conviction is involved an objective situation which gives. the religious statements their factual or cognitive force. Now, this must be made clear that the convictor, the objective situation, present in the case of religion is not objective in the same sense in which scientific or ordinary factual situations are. The objective situation present before the religious man is objective only for those who look to the world and life with a specific conviction, or, in other words, who share the conviction. of the convictus. The objectivity of the religious situation is not verifiable and falsifiable in the same public way in which scientific objectivity is. Zuurdeeg, although much conscious of distinguishing scientific (or indicative) language from convictional language, somewhat confuses the issue of objectivity involved in the two kinds of languages when he says, "It is not the analytic philosopher's business to decide whether the reality meant in a certain language is 'really' there or not. The only thing he can do is to notice that if human beings speak either indicative or convictional language, they refer to something which is *'real for them'*."[47] The expression *'real for them'* used in both the cases may create a confusion. Religious factuality is never similar to scientific factuality. Schmidt seems more straightforward and clearer in this regard when, after taking the problem of cognitivity or factuality of statements from chapter to chapter in his above-mentioned book, he concludes that religious statements can't be factual in the scientific sense, or, as he says, the former can never have a knowledge-by-description claim like the scientific statements.

We fully appreciate Schmidt's genius so far as he very ably shows that religious statements cannot claim a factuality similar to that of scientific statements. But this conclusion, we think, does not forthwith open before one a path to interpret religious statements in purely dispositional terms so that the factual force behind these statements may become something simply deceptive and misleading. At least this cannot be done if one takes into consideration the use of these statements as made by the religious believers themselves. It cannot be said that through these statements the believers want simply to express or evoke-invoke certain pervasive dispositions. Religious statements have some point behind their cognitive form. They have got an objectivity of their own special kind. Schmidt, no doubt, fully acknowledges the value and worth of religious experiences for the person or persons who have them, and therefore it seems. to us that he, unlike many others, is not absolutely deaf to the point behind the factual and descriptive force of the religious statements. He clearly charges the sceptics of a grave fault when they take such experiences as mere illusions. He is also prepared to say that such experiences generate attitudes, foster pervasive patterns of behaviour.[48] But then he takes these experiences as purely private and psychological and hence the religious statements, if they are at all to be taken factually, as the reports of purely private feelings. He gives these experiences psychological value, but no cognitive value. As is clear from his statement, "Faced with a deep moral perplexity in which each alternative course of action seems to leave us in a hopeless situation, one may feel god's presence. Or, awakening on a spring morning amidst a gorgeous display of nature far away from all other humans, one may feel his presence. But, given such situations and others, what we cannot succeed in doing is to point out within the situation the specific referent on which attention is to be focussed ......"[49] And Schmidt concludes for the man who has such experiences that what he has felt is private.

But here we have to submit that if by taking religious experiences as private, Schmidt means that these experiences do not occur to those who do not possess a specific conviction or faith towards world and life, he is perfectly correct and we do agree with him. But if by taking the experiences as private, he means to take them as simple individual possessions, as certain reflections and projections of one's mind, we will perhaps not agree with him. We believe that there is something in the world-and-life situation itself which makes the believer sometimes have some experience which is known as religious experience. Of course, this 'something' is not open to all in the fashion of an ordinary scientific 'fact', but it is open to all those who share the specific conviction with which the believer looks towards world and life. Schmidt says that the religious man can point to no referent. But we feel that he can and he does. It is not a fact that when one sees a God 'amidst the gorgeous display of nature', he has no referent there to point to. The referent is there, although not in the fashion of a scientific referent, and is open to all those who share the conviction of the man who sees God. They can all verify his statement that 'there is a God in the gorgeous display' for themselves with reference to the experience they all share. Schmidt seems to give religious experience, in as much as the cognitive claim is concerned, a status even worse than the feeling of a toothache or the feeling of someone being followed by a ghost in the darkness of the night. He says that in both these cases there are concrete referents with reference to which the statements can be verified or falsified. Public checks are possible in both the cases. In the former case a dentist can check the truth of the statement 'I feel toothache' by finding the presence of a cavity in one of the teeth. Similarly, in the latter case also, there are public checks possible for verifying whether the statement 'I feel someone is following me' is true or not. It may be that even after public checks in which it has been found that the man is being followed by none, he may retain the feeling, but that is another point. What counts here is that his statement is capable of public check and the factual claims made therein are capable of being verified or falsified.

But in religious statements based on the feeling of God's presence in one's experience, there is no such referent with reference to which the statement is to be verified or falsified.

But here what we want to submit is that, although it is not clear to us whether religious statements are really to be assimilated with the statements about the feeling of a toothache, or about a delusional experience, this much we can point out with certainty that religious statements also have referent and with reference to that they may be checked and verified. Of course, such a verification is not open to all, but again it is not simply confined to only one man or two. The referent is open to all those who share the religious faith or who have the religious eye. Religious statements, we may say, have an 'odd' kind of referent. If asked for a referent, the religious man may point to the things which are even empirically present to us. He may point to the world around us, to the life as a whole, to the starry heaven above, to a beautiful spring morning, to all natural beauties and all that, and try to make one show his God there. It is possible that one may not see his God in those objects, but then he is pointing to a fact which is fully objective to him. He may even point to ordinary physical objects for his referent of the religious statements. These objects may be certain stones, or images, or trees, or certain such other objects. Certain personalities like Ram, Krishna, Jesus, Buddha etc. invariably serve as the referents of the ordinary man's religious statements. But again, by pointing to these he is not pointing to hard objective and historical facts. The facts looked at, as they are, are scientific facts. It is only when they are looked at with a special conviction that a God implied therein is seen. Similarly, Ram, Krishna etc. taken as hard historical beings are scientific facts and as these they do not form the referent, but these facts looked at with a specific conviction form the referents of the religious statements. Similarly, the world and life by themselves do not form the referent, but looked at with a specific 'blik', as Hare would call it, something 'more', something unique is seen in them which forms the referent of the religious statements.

Further, the truths of religious experience are certainly not communicable, as Schmidt rightly says, to those 'who have not experienced it', but they are perfectly communicable with full meaning amongst those who share the same conviction.

Because religious experiences are not communicable to those who have not experienced them, they do not become something simply private. They are certainly not comparable to scientific experiences but they are perfectly comparable to aesthetic experiences. Beauty is not something objective to which one may point. But still when one says something to be beautiful, or that when he sees beauty in a thing, he is not expressing simply his private experience or feeling. He is pointing to something which has got some objective status too. A beautiful object is not 'beauty', but still it serves as a referent for beauty for the man who sees beauty in it and who can make it see to all those who share his conviction towards the object. We shall try to clarify these points further in our coming chapter, but here what we are anxious to press home is the point that the factual force behind the religious statements and the alleged objective content of religious experiences are not something purely private and subjective. They have certainly not a scientific factuality but they have got what we have been calling convictional factuality. Religious statements are the reports of convictions, and convictions, we repeat, are never merely subjective. They are based on objective considerations and they also reveal objective facts which are incapable of being revealed without the conviction.[50] Convictional facts, although not as factual as scientific, are still fully objective for all those who are bound by a common conviction. Religious experiences have not only a psychological value, but a cognitive value too, of course, in their own ways. This cognitivity is only convictional and relative.

### v. Religious Statements as 'Blik'-statements

Such a view has been very characteristically expressed by R.M. Hare in his reaction against A. Flew's challenge to religion in terms of his (the latter's) falsifiability criterion. Hare wants to point out that religious statements are not assertions, they do not assert facts, rather they express the inner conviction or attitude of the believer in relation to the world. Now, such an attitude which the religious believer expresses towards the world through his statements are unchangeable in any circumstance whatsoever. They are exceptionally enduring. To express this non-falsifiable, non-changeable character of the religious attitude, Hare uses a special term 'blik', and says that religious statements are blik-statements. A blik is nothing but, as Gibson says, a 'confirmed way of looking at things'.[52] And hence, religious statements as expressing the blik of the believer express his confirmed way of looking towards the world. Hare illustrates his point by means of a parable about a lunatic who is convinced that the dons want to murder him. To remove such a 'blik' of the lunatic towards dons, certain such dons are presented to him who are perfectly harmless and kind to him, but still he does not change his opinion about them and says about one such, "Yes, but that was only his diabolical cunning; he's really plotting against me all the time, like the rest of them."[53] What does the lunatic's attitude towards the dons show? That he is not going to change his conviction about them whatsoever contrary instances he might come across. Similar is the case with the religious man's assertion of religious statements that 'God exists', 'God is love' etc. In uttering these statements, he is expressing such a deep-rooted conviction that he is hardly prepared to give them up in face of any contradictory circumstance. These statements are expressing his 'blik' towards the world like one that the lunatic expresses towards the dons.

In giving such an analysis of religious statements, Hare is really depicting a great truth. Religious statements by their very nature, for reasons already advanced, cannot be said to be factual statements. They express inner conviction or attitude of the believer towards the world. But again, characterising religious statements as purely attitudinal with no further implications makes them something purely psychological and irrational. Religious attitude on such an analysis comes to be nothing more than an insane, irrational, subjective attitude towards the world. Such a nature of them is all the more confirmed in Hare's analysis by his comparison of the religious attitude with the insane lunatic's blik towards the dons. But will Hare himself be prepared for a literal comparison of the religious blik with the lunatic's insane blik? Certainly not. He distinguishes between 'sane' and 'insane' bliks and wants to categorise religious bliks under the former. This shows that he wants to press the comparison only to that extent which shows that religious 'bliks' are hardly changeable and falsifiable. By the parable he draws on, he simply wants to present the non-hypothetical, non-tentative character of the religious statements and nothing more. What he wants, in our view, to show by having a distinction between 'sane' and 'insane' 'right' and 'wrong' blik and putting the religious one under the former, is that religious blik, although unalterable like the neurotic's blik, is nevertheless not irrational, neurotic, and hysteric like the latter. The former may be called *non-rational*, but not *irrational*. And the word 'non-rational' shows that although religious 'bliks' cannot be justified on logical or rational grounds, they must have some such other ground which may justly be called rational as contrasted to irrational. To quote John Wisdom's words, the reason for the religious belief may not be like the 'links of a chain', but it must be something like the 'legs of a chair'.[54]

It is certainly unfortunate on Hare's part that he did not analyse the full implications of his blik-theory so as to explain the rationality (as opposed to irrationality) of the religious blik. And it is this drawback which has provoked certain criticisms from certain quarters against his distinction between 'sane' and 'insane' bliks. It is pointed out that if the lunatic's blik towards the dons is an insane blik, as Hare calls it, what will be the sane 'blik' towards them? It will certainly be one which will allow certain instances as going against it and in that case in Hare's own sense of the word "blik", it will no longer be entitled to be called a blik at all.[55] But in our view such a criticism miserably misses Hare's point in such a distinction. This is clear from Hare's unambiguous statement that there cannot be a distinction between 'blik' and 'no blik', but it can only be between a 'sane' and an 'insane' blik.[56] By 'sane' and 'insane', he does not mean 'falsifiable' and unfalsifiable', but something like 'healthy' and 'unhealthy', 'good' and 'bad', 'approvable' and 'non-approvable. The other kind of blik that one may have towards the dons will be equally unfalsifiable in character; only it may be more healthy, more approvable than the lunatic's one and it is in that sense that it will be called 'sane' as contrasted to insane'. It is in this sense that Hare calls the religious blik as 'right' or 'sane' and implies thereby that religious bliks have got some rationality about them. As we have said above, Hare does not develop this aspect of his blik-theory in the essay mentioned above and it is perhaps for completing this imperfect task that he takes up again a discussion of religious statements in his another essay Religion & Morals.[57] There he tries to show that besides the purely attitudinal element, the religious statements imply certain factual elements too and that is how religious statements get a factual or cognitive force behind them and thus do not remain purely psychological or prescriptive. While seeing some object with an attitude of worship, for example, we do not simply impose some subjective choice of ours on the object, rather we actually see something there in the object which evokes such an attitude in us and while worshipping the object with that attitude, we have certain expectations too. These considerations show that religious beliefs are not merely attitudinal, but also in some sense factual.

## REFERENCES

1. R. Carnap, *'Philosophy & Logical Syntax'*, Chapter I, quoted here from Alston & Nakhnikian's (ed.) *'Twentieth Century Philosophy'* (where the whole Chapter is reprinted), p. 432.

2. Included in *'Metaphysical Beliefs'* (London, S.C.M. Press, 1957) edited by A.C. MacIntyre and R.G. Smith.

3. A.C. MacIntyre, 'The Logical Status of Religious Belief' in ibid., p. 182.

4. Ibid., p. 209.

5. Ibid., p. 202.

6. Like Braithwaite & Hepburn, MacIntyre also takes religious language to be mythical & moral to a great extent and he speaks of religious language as a language of total commitment to a "form of life" but as to religious statements, i.e. statements about God, he accepts that they are descriptive and for them he presents the above analysis.

7. A. MacIntyre, ibid., p. 196.

8. Ibid., p. 185.

9. B. Mitchell, 'The Justification of Religious Belief', *Philosophical Quarterly*, July 1961, p. 219.

10. Howard Root, 'Metaphysics and Religious Beliefs' in *Prospects for Metaphysics*, edited by Ian T. Ramsey, p. 76.

11. R.B. Braithwaite, *'An Empiricist's View of the Nature of Religious Belief'* (Cambridge University Press, 1955), quoted here from an excerpt from the above book included in Abernethy & Langford's (ed,) book *'Philosophy of Religion'*, p. 352.

12. Ibid., p. 353.

13. Ibid., p. 357.

14. R.W. Hepburn, *'Christianity & Paradox'* (C.A. Watts & Co., London, 1958), p. 192.

15. Ibid.

16. Ibid., p. 193.

17. R.M. Hare, 'Religion & Morals' included in B. Mitchell's (ed.) *Faith and Logic*, p. 179.

18. Ibid., p. 180.

19. R.B. Braithwaite in op. cit. Quoted here from an excerpt from Braithwaite's book included in John Hick's (ed.) *'The Existence of God'* (New York, MacMillan, 1964), p. 235.

20. R.W. Hepburn, p. 195, in op. cit.

21. Ibid., p. 193.

22. T.R. Miles, *'Religion and Scientific Outlook'* (George Allen & Unwin, London, 1959), pp. 39ff.

23. Ibid., p. 166.

24. TIbid., p. 169.

25. Ibid., p. 179.

26. Ibid., p. 179.

27. Ibid., p. 163.

28. John Wisdom, "Gods", in A. Flew's (ed.) *'Logic & Language'*, 1st series, p. 197.

29. William E. Kennick, 'The Language of Religion', *Philosophical Review*, Vol. 65, 1956, p. 66.

30. Ibid., p. 66.

31. Ibid., p. 68.

32. Paul F. Schmidt, *'Religious Knowledge'* (Free Pree of Glancoe, 1961), p. ix of the preface.

33. Ibid., p. 95.

34. Ibid., p. 77.

35. Ibid., p. 76.
36. Ibid., pp. 76-77.
37. Ibid., p. 76.
38. Ibid., p. 95.
39. Ibid., p. 92.
40. Ibid.
41. Ibid.
42. Ibid.
43. Ibid., p. 111.
44. William F. Zuurdeeg, 'An Analytic Philosophy of Religion' (George Allen & Unwin, London, 1959), pp. 25-26.
45. Ibid., p. 29.
46. Ibid., pp. 26 & 45.
47. Ibid., p. 45.
48. By way of charging the sceptic who is not prepared to give any value to the religious experiences, Schmidt says: "Why make the reverse error of trying to destroy the feeling because the descriptive claim does not hold good?.... It would be a mistake to lose the feelings of such experience if one has them ; they are one of the riches of life; they too, can generate attitudes and constitute pervasive patterns of behaviour and explain the meanings of religious assertions." Op. cit., pp. 129-31.
49. Ibid., p. 127.

50. Zuurdeeg is perfectly right when he says: "People who are in grip of convictions... can often open our eyes... The service rendered by convictional to indicative language can be described as the blasting away of an obstruction, which prevented people from seeing clearly in an indicative way." Op. cit., p. 53.

51. R.M. Hare, "Theology & Falsification' (B) in *New Essays etc*.

52. A. Boyce Gibson, 'Modern Philosophers consider Religion', *Australasian Journal of Philosophy*, Vol. 35, No. 3, pp. 171.

53. Hare, ibid., p. 100.

54. John Wisdom, op. cit.

55. William T. Blackstone, *'The Problem of Religious Knowledge'* (Prentice Hall, 1963), p. 77. Also Duff-Forbes, Theology and Falsification Again' in op. cit., p, 145.

56. Hare, op. cit, p. 100.

57. Included in Basil Mitchell's (ed.) ' *Faith and Logic'*.

# 5
# TRUE NATURE OF RELIGIOUS BELIEF—AUTHOR'S VIEW

We have thus seen that there are two kinds of approaches in contemporary philosophy, one virtually opposed to the other, regarding the nature of religious belief. The one approach takes God-statements as literally or perfectly factual, while the other takes them as non-factual. We have found that there are difficulties with regard to both the approaches. How then to find out the true nature of religious belief? The terms factual-non-factual' or 'cognitive-non-cognitive' are mutually exclusive and therefore, if there are difficulties in taking religious belief as either factual or non-factual, how else can its nature be defined? We have perhaps to be satisfied with the opinion that, as Goa is a mystery, so also religious belief is a mystery and its nature cannot be properly deciphered. But the situation is not so hopeless and there is, we hope, ample scope and opportunity to decipher the true nature of religious belief, if we try to analyse and understand the nature of the utterances made by the religious believers a bit more closely and faithfully. The two opposing analyses have proved to be defective, because they have been one sided in their approach. Both of them have laid exclusive emphasis upon only one of the two features exhibited by religious man's utterances to the utter neglect of the other.

A true meaning of the religious statements, and hence a true nature of religious belief, can be deciphered only if both of these features are given due attention and regard.

Now, therefore, we will have to see what those two features are which we are talking about and how each side has been guilty of attending to only one of them with an utter disregard for the other. The two features that we are talking about and that we are going to mention just now are not something new or original. They are rather well implicit in the considerations we have made so far. Religious man's statement of his religious belief exhibits two obvious features— (1) He utters his statements with full factual force and all his behaviours (religious acts) testify to his taking the statements as perfectly factual, (2) He sticks to his statements with a sense of commitment such that in no circumstances he is ready to accept his statements falsified. Now, these two features of religious statements are obviously contradictory. A statement cannot be both factual and non-falsifiable at the same time. Perhaps this is why contemporary thinkers have taken sides and have tended to accept only one of the two features. Our simple logic says that one of the two alternatives must be true, although both cannot be true at the same time. Thinkers belonging to the first trend make most out of the first characteristic and totally neglect the second. Similarly, thinkers belonging to the second trend make most out of the second characteristic and totally neglect the first one. And hence both are guilty of one-sidedness. The former forget that, if while expressing his religious belief through some of his seemingly factual statements, the religious men were uttering statements of the ordinary factual nature, he must have readily allowed the possibility of his statements being falsified by certain conceivable empirical situations. But we find that he is never ready to do so. He asserts his statements with a full sense of commitment and takes them compatible with each and every situation. This should be an ample evidence of the fact that even by uttering statements of the factual form, the religious man is not uttering factual statements of the ordinary nature and it is futile, or rather misconceived, to compare his statements with ordinary factual statements or scientific statements which are of the nature of hypotheses always liable to be falsified. The latter, who on the strength that religious statements are not falsifiable go straightway to the characterisation of these statements as non-factual and begin to present thoroughly indirect analysis of them, forget that if while expressing his belief the religious men were, for instance, merely expressing his allegiance to a particular behaviour policy, as Braithwaite says, then why should he use factual statements, why should he not have expressed his belief in certain clear-cut moral maxims? They think that the factual form of his statements has got absolutely no meaning. Perhaps they think that the factual form of these statements is product of some sort of illusion on the part of the religious believers. But what right might an analyst have to characterise religious man's assertion of his statements as factual to be illusory? Perhaps this, that he does not allow his statements to be falsified. But does this fact straightway pave the way for an analyst to characterise the factual form of the religious statements as illusory? To our mind, not. The religious man might have his own reasons in asserting his statements as factual and yet sticking to them with a sense of commitment. Taking the factual form of his statements as simply illusory is not really explaining his position in its true nature, rather it is explaining that away. The religious man must not be treated like a babbling child who babbles without knowing that he is babbling. He might be fully conscious of the position he stands on, and we will simply fail to appreciate his position properly, if we characterise the factual form of his statements as illusory in an *a-priori* way. Braithwaite remarks against the logical positivists who take religious statements as expressions of certain feelings, "Few religious men would be prepared to admit that their religion was merely a matter of feelings: feelings may enter into their religions, but to evince such feelings is certainly not the primary use of their religious assertions."[1] But does Braithwaite ever realise that the same sort of objection applies to his views also? Would any religious man be ever prepared to accept that his religion was merely a matter of morality, or that his religious belief was merely a repository of certain moral ideas? Braithwaite realises, and quite correctly, that any analyst of religious statements must keep in his mind the way in which the religious man uses and understands his statements. But it is rather pathetic to note that while he realises this truth in criticising the logical positivists, he forgets it completely when he comes to propound his own theory. Truly, any analysis of religious statements must keep it in close touch with the use of these statements as made by the religious believers. Words and expressions do not mean by themselves. It is their users who mean something by their use. It is possible that the religious people by the use of their statements in the way they do might be referring to something very significant, which we have been miserably missing due to certain straight jackets that we have formed in the light of our ordinary logic and want things to fit in them. The theologians might be misrepresenting the whole truth behind the factual form of the religious statements by comparing them with scientific statements and by advancing proofs for establishing their factuality, but yet the religious man might be standing on a very sound, reasonable and understandable position in asserting his statements in the factual form and yet not allowing them to be falsified.

Thus, in our view, if we are really sincere to find out the real logic of the religious man's belief, we have to be more faithful to his way of expressing his belief than to our ordinary logic. Understanding the nature of religious belief does not mean prescribing something from one's own side keeping in view the laws of ordinary logic. We have rather to find out the logic of the belief itself in a neutral manner by going deep into it and by keeping close to the characteristics that it manifests or exhibits. In making any analysis of the nature of religious belief, we must do justice to both of the above characteristics of the religious man's assertion of his faith. We must go into the explanation of why the religious man holds on to his belief in seemingly opposed ways.

We have yet to see, however, whether any such analysis of the religious statements may be advanced which may make proper sense out of both the characteristics of the religious statements that we have mentioned above. We believe that it may be done and we are going to try the same in the following pages.

Keeping all aspects of the problem in view, we find it most reasonable to suggest that the religious man's belief (i.e., religious belief) is the result of his being very strongly impressed by the universe as a whole in a specific way, and his statements are the expressions of his this strong and total impression about the universe. We hope to prove in due course that this way of understanding the nature of religious belief does ample justice to the two ways in which the religious man uses his statements and also it becomes able to find a significant sense in the two seemingly opposed ways in which the religious man asserts his belief. But first of all, let us analyse our suggestion and try to make the points involved in it clear. We have to make clear our two expressions: (1) 'being very strongly impressed in a specific way' and (2) 'the universe as a whole'. Let us first take the second expression, viz., 'universe as a whole'.

As a matter of fact, the notion of the universe as a whole is somewhat troublesome. In contemporary philosophy, empiricists like Russell, Paul Edwards etc. seem to have held the notion as meaningless. According to them the notion of as a whole is a purely subjective one and has got no objective status of its own. It signifies nothing other than a mere sum-total of the parts. But when we talk here about the universe as whole, we do not mean a bare mechanical sum-total of the different parts of the universe. When traditionally it has been said that philosophy is a study of the nature of the universe as a whole, while science is a study of its specific parts or aspects, it does not follow therefrom that philosophical study is a sum-total of the different scientific studies. The notion of as-a-whole is different here from the mere sum-total of parts. Even if all the different specific aspects in all their details are studied by the different sciences, there still remains a significance of the study of the universe as a whole, which philosophy, at least in its traditional nature, has been trying to study. The overall picture that one forms of an object containing parts by having a general look around it is different from the picture that one forms of the object by looking to its parts in details and then summing them up. Similarly, the notion of universe as a whole is a notion different from that of the sum-total of the different parts of the universe. And it has its own significance. It is not something purely imaginary and meaningless, as empiricists have generally tried to suggest. The notion may not have any strict scientific significance, but it has got a meaning and a use in the sphere of morality, aesthetics and religion. If there are certain lines drawn on a sheet of paper or on a blackboard, for example, and one looks to the lines piecemeal and adds them in his mind, he will have some specific kind of perception or experience. But again, if he looks to the lines not separately, but somehow taking them together in one range of vision, or as a whole, he will have a different experience, an experience not merely of the jumble of a few lines, but of a gestalt, a configuration, which will present a definite image before him of, say, a bird, or a star, or a flower, or something like that. Similarly, when one looks to the different parts of a face separately—the nose, the eye, the ear etc.- and tries to have an impression thereof on the basis of his perception of the parts, the impression will certainly be different from one which be forms by looking to the face as a whole in one broad vision. The notion of as-a-whole thus does not lock to be a superfluous notion. It has sense and significance. John Hick has very ably tried to clarify the notion of as-a-whole in his book *Faith and Knowledge*[2] by citing the example of a situation in which a man suddenly entered into a room where a rehearsal for a drama was going on. The man really entered these to save himself from certain miscreants who were chasing him. But first when he entered the room and saw in it men with long beards and armed with lethal weapons like sword, bear etc., he was all the more frightened to find him in the hands of still more dangerous people. But when after a moment he gathered some courage and looked to the situation as a whole with some patience, he immediately read a new meaning in the situation. He realised that it was a dressing room and the people there were all members of a drama party. So long as he viewed the situation in parts, he had a different impressing, but the moment he looked to the situation as a whole, the picture changed; all the same things appeared to him in a different light altogether.

All these illustrations go to show that in spite of the negative attitude of the empiricists, the notion of as-a-whole is a significant one and it is different from the notion of a mere sum-total of parts. Of course, there is a vital difference between an as-a-whole experience of ordinary things and situations and that of the entire universe. In the former case, all the parts are fully visible, but in the latter case, the entire range of the different parts is never visible. There is thus a difficulty in understanding the notion of the universe as a whole on the analogy of the ordinary as-a-whole experiences. Nevertheless, we must emphasize that the analogies show that the notion of the universe as a whole is not a meaningless notion and it has got some kind of objectivity. The universe as a whole signifies a general picture of the universe formed out of the entire set of empirical evidences-past and present-that one has regarding the nature and character of the universe.

Let us now come to the notion of being very strongly impressed in a specific way'. Being impressed by something in a specific way is not the same as having a simple cognition of that thing. It is not cognition, rather it is an affective product of the cognition. It implies the experience of an additional dimension in the perceptual data presented by the object. It is like a value-experience in which the value-quality pervades the entire object of perception. Two persons may not be impressed in the same way by the same perceptual data presented before them. One may be impressed in one specific way while the other may be impressed in another specific way. One may experience one kind of additional dimension, one kind of new quality pervading all over, while the other may either completely miss it or experience some other kind of pervading value-quality. Let us try to understand the whole thing by means of an illustration. When we call an object, say, a rose or a picture, beautiful, what is it that we are really expressing. Or, to understand it a bit different, what is it that we see in the object that makes us call it beautiful? Is beauty a quality of the object like (or over and above) such other empirical qualities as yellowness, softness etc. that we perceive in the object in the process of our ordinary cognition of it? Certainly not. Then what is it? It is an affective product of our cognition of the object; it is a result of our being impressed by the object in a specific way, or in other words, it is the way in which we have been impressed by the object. In being impressed by the object in this way which has prompted us to call it beautiful, we have found a new dimension in the object, have experienced a value-quality pervading the entire object of our perception. It is not necessary, however, that everybody perceiving the object is impressed by it in the same way. There may be others who miss this new dimension of the object and may be impressed by it somewhat differently which may incite them either to deny the presence of beauty in the object or else to call it ugly. Thus with the same object in sight two people may be impressed by it in two different ways.

Now, if we apply the above analysis to one's experience of the universe as a whole, we may see that there may be a sense in which one may be said to have been impressed by it in one specific way, while the other is impressed in another specific way. Being impressed by the universe as a whole in one specific way implies, on the above analogy, having experience of an additional dimension in it, a new value-quality pervading although the data ordinarily presented by it to the senses. With the same sort of data presented to us all by the universe, as it actually does, we may not be all impressed by it in the same way. Some of us may be impressed by it in one specific way, the theistic way, so to say, while others may be affected or impressed by it in another specific way, the atheistic way. Consequently, some of us are theists while other are atheists. We have said above that being impressed by something in a specific way implies experiencing an additional dimension, a new quality in the object. Thus while the theist or the religious believer becomes impressed by the universe as a whole in the theistic way, he experiences an additional dimension, a new value-quality permeating every cell of the universe, as it were. This additional dimension or the all-pervading value-quality that he experiences, he terms 'God'. The atheist misses this experience and has a different picture of the universe as a whole before him in the same way in which a man fails to see beauty in an object or a particular configuration in a set of lines. God, thus, is a value-quality pervading the entire universe in the same sense in which beauty is the value-quality pervading the entire object called beautiful. Religious experience or God-experience is the experience of a divine quality pervading throughout the universe. It is not the experience of an individual person over and above the universe before us, rather it is the experience of an overriding quality running throughout the universe itself. And the experience of this additional quality in the universe is the result of the individual being impressed by it in a specific way, the theistic way as we call it. Theism and atheism both are thus the results of two different sorts of impressions that people form about the universe as a whole, or in other words, of the two ways in which they are impressed by the universe as a whole. Such overall impressions about the universe as a whole we may call total impressions and in that language we may say that both theistic and atheistic beliefs are the results of two different sorts of total impressions about the universe.

Now such impressions are total not only in the sense that they are formed with regard to the total universe. They are total in a different, and rather a more important, sense also. We have said about the nature of religious belief not only that it is the result of being impressed by the universe as a whole in a specific way, but also that it is the result of being *very strongly* impressed by the universe in that specific way. The use of the expression 'very strongly' is also very significant here and that will have to be explained and analysed. Religious impressions are not the ordinary sort of impressions that we so often form in our daily life about persons or objects and change them so often. Of course, to understand the nature of such impressions, we have drawn an analogy or comparison between them and the impression regarding beauty or gestalt-formation. But there is a very vital difference between the two situations. In other words, the ordinary impressions that we form in our daily life are very different in nature from the impression that we form about the universe as a whole. The two different impressions that we form in relation to the universe make very vital difference in the life and existence situations of the two persons who have them. Such impressions are not ordinary impressions. They make vital impact upon our life. They, to use the language of Paul Tillich, concern us ultimately. Religion, says, Tillich, is a matter of 'ultimate concern'[3]. This ultimate concern is very different from ordinary concerns, because with it are associated the questions of not this or that fact nor of this or that aspect of life, but the fundamental. questions related with the world as a whole or life as a whole, such as, the questions of the origin and end of the world, the questions of life and death, the questions of the existence and ultimate destiny and so on. Tillich has distinguished in his. book *Systematic Theology (Vol. I)* between ordinary (pre-liminary, as Tillich calls it) and ultimate concerns and has pointed out that while the former are partial, conditional and tentative, the latter is total, unconditional and absolute.[4] Thus our ultimate concern is our total concern also, because with it are associated the questions of our very life and death. Because it is in such deep and intense situations or moments of life (in which man is deeply concerned with certain fundamental questions relating to world and life) that man is impressed by the universe in a specific way, his impression is. very much deep-rooted and affects not only this or that aspect of life, but really the total life, the total man. The man is, as it were, shaken from within. He is, to use the words of W.F. Zuurdeeg, 'convicted', 'strongly got hold of', 'overwhelmed' and 'overpowered'.[5] Thus, being very strongly impressed by the universe in a specific way means here being impressed in a total, pervasive and fundamental way such that. the life of the impressed man is shaken from within, it gets a. new twist altogether and the man becomes deeply overpowered by a light, a dimension, which he cannot very easily forsake or forget. This may amply tell us of the non-tentative, non-falsifiable character of the religious belief. The convicted man changes from within and his feelings, thought and deed are all strongly affected by the impression that he has.

But a question will naturally arise here: why is not every one of us impressed by the universe in the same way? The universe is what it is and therefore naturally it presents the same set of data to all of us alike. Then why the difference in impression? Why are some of us impressed in the theistic way while others in the atheistic way? One answer to the question may be given by simply citing the analogy of the impression of beauty in an object.

Just as, it may be said, in the same object some experience beauty, while others do not, similarly some of us have an experience of a divine colour in the universe while others do not have any such experience. Or to take another analogy, it may be said that just as in the same set of lines one person sees one sort of configuration or gestalt, while another person sees another sort of gestalt or configuration, similarly in the same set of data presented by the universe, one person sees a God while the other does not see. But perhaps this may not be taken as a complete answer. The same question may be asked regarding the experience of beauty or the experience of a particular gestalt itself. It may be asked in general: why, after all, such differences in impression, when the data presented are the same? And now we will have to advance to a more basic level to answer the question. An answer may be borrowed here from John Hick which he has developed in his book *Faith and Knowledge*. Hick would say here that the different impressions are due to different interpretations made by the persons concerned. The data, which Hick terms in his own terminology as 'significance', are of course the same but the interpretations are different and hence the persons concerned are differently impressed. In every knowledge-situation Hick distinguishes between two factors-a significance and an interpretation, and according to him experiences of the same significance differ due to different interpretations.[6] But we find that even despite this answer the question raised at the beginning of the paragraph may be asked over again in the same form: Why, different interpretations?

And once again we have come to the same point. We will have to seek, therefore, for the most basic answer. Such an answer in our view is that, people are impressed differently because they look to the object with two different convictions or attitudes. Looked at with one particular attitude, the universe, presents itself as divinised or God-ful, so to say, but looked at with a different attitude, it presents itself as a bare world. By using Hare's phrase we can say that the universe looked at with a particular *bilk* it presents itself as a bare physical world. Thus theistic and atheistic beliefs are the results of two different total impressions formed about the total universe due to viewing towards it with two different *bliks*.

But now another question comes up regarding the nature and status of these attitudes themselves. What is the status of these attitudes? Are they some pre-possessions of the mind? For, it will be said, had it not been so, there could not have been such a basic difference in attitudes of persons. Thus, in the first instance it seems that the answer to the question must be affirmative. And if really it is affirmative, it will have far reaching implications. If the attitudes are purely subjective in the sense of being certain pre-possessions having elements of wishful thinking, then the religious experience of a new dimension in the universe will be something purely subjective, having no objective significance. In a sense the attitudes are certainly subjective, because they differ from one person to another, but they are not so in the sense that they are purely imaginary or created by the person within him in vacuum. To our mind, they are rather formed and strengthened to a very great extent by our beliefs and cognitions themselves. We develop attitudes gradually in the light of our beliefs, experiences and cognitions themselves. A religious sort of attitude is formed under the impact of our religious beliefs and cognitions themselves.

But in saying all these we are obviously lapsing into a vicious circularity. We have said above that our religious belief or religious experience is the result of a specific attitude, or conviction or bilk. And now we are saying that this blik or attitude is formed under the impact of our beliefs, experiences and cognitions themselves. So we are obviously arguing in a circle. But we think that this circularity cannot be avoided here, because it seems to be a necessary part of the uniqueness of the religious situation. It is difficult to say which comes first-belief or attitude. John Hick in the introduction of his book *Faith and Knowledge* distinguishes in a similar context between what he calls 'faith as cognition' and 'faith as trust'[7] His faith as cognition is more or less the same as what we are calling belief, and his faith as trust is more or less the same as what we are calling conviction or blik. Hick is of opinion that faith as trust depends upon faith as cognition, because according to him unless we have a vision, a direct cognition, we cannot have conviction, i.e., we cannot develop a blik or a confirmed attitude. And Hick seems correct in so far as he goes. But he misses the point that faith as cognition also as much depends upon faith as trust as the latter depends upon the former. Unless we approach the universe with a specific blik or conviction, a specific cognition or vision cannot be had. We have seen that we have the vision of a new dimension in the universe only when we look to the universe with a specific blik. So the two are interwined in such a close relationship that it cannot be said distinctly which depends upon which and which is prior to which. The two seem to go *pari passu* and it cannot be said decisively whether belief (vision or experience) comes first or the conviction comes first. The following lines of John Ballie seem to be very appropriate here, "This is a region of experience in which there can be no apprehension without commitment, but it is equally true to say that there can be no commitment without apprehension." The words 'apprehension' and 'commitment' here are more or less equivalents of the word 'cognition' (belief), and 'conviction' (or 'blik' or 'specific attitude') as used by us. The circularity thus shows the uniqueness of the religious situation which cannot be compared to ordinary cognitive situations.

To return now to our main point again that the religious belief is the result of being very strongly impressed by the universe as a whole, we shall have to realise that the new dimension or the value-quality that we experience in course of such a strong impression has a fairly objective status in its own unique way and it cannot be regarded as something purely subjective. The vision or experience of the new dimension in the universe is like a discernment or discovery made, which persons lacking in the specific blik fail to make. When we see beauty in an object, it is of course true that beauty does not belong to the object in the same sense in which other empirical qualities like yellowness, softness etc. belong to it. But still it cannot be said that beauty is a purely subjective quality imposed on to the object by our mind. Because it is said that beauty is the result of our being impressed by the object in a particular way, it is natural to be inclined to take it as a purely subjective quality. But this inclination is not adequate and proper. Closer examination will reveal that although beauty is not a state-of-affair given out there in the external object, still it is not something purely subjective. It is only when the object is seen with a specific attitude that it looks beautiful, but, as we have seen at least in the religious context, attitudes are not something purely subjective. Our attitudes are formed in the light of our beliefs and experiences themselves. It will have to be accepted that within the various dimensions of the objéct itself there is something which somehow impresses the observer in a way which makes him call the object beautiful. Thus in its own way beauty has got an objective status. This relative objectivity of beauty is further confirmed and strengthened by the fact that an object which impresses one man in the way which makes him call it beautiful impresses many other in the same way. The rose flower, for example, looks beautiful to most of us. So, unless there be something somehow present in the empirical features of the object itself, how could most of us unanimously see beauty in the same object? Of course, the object will look beautiful only to that majority which will look to it with a common attitude or conviction, and not to all, but still a majority of people being impressed by an object in the same way testifies to a great extent the truth of the fact that the beauty that one sees in an object is not purely subjective if not perfectly objective. In seeing beauty in the object we discern or discover a new dimension in it which has an objective depth in its own right. Because its discernment or discovery involves a specific attitude on the part of the observer, it does not mean that the discovery is illusory or subjective. The following lines of Zuurdeeg seem to be very relevantly significant here, "People possessed of strong convictions may often observe something which have indicative meaning and which has been overlooked."[8] Or again, as John Wisdom very significantly re-marks, "Discoveries have been made not only by Christopher Columbus and Pasteur, but also by Tolstoy and Pasteur, but also by Tolstoy and Dostievsky and Freud. Things are revealed to us not only by scientist with microscopes, but also by poets, prophets and painters."[9] That is, what is discerned or discovered by people of a certain attitude or conviction is not something illusory, it has also got some significance and value. Discoveries made by people of strong convictions may not be available to common observers, but still they are discoveries and they have their meaning. They are objective and factual in their own ways. So, when a religious man discerns a new dimension in the universe by looking to it with his specific attitude and conviction, it is not that he is 'engrossed in a passion'. He has found something objective in the universe which people without that conviction have miserably missed. He has made a discovery which has an objective depth and reality. This is why he relates the fruit of his experience in cognitive or factual statements. And there is a meaningful communicability amongst all those who have such experiences about the nature of these experiences through the statements made by them. The logician may fail to understand how the statements could be cognitively meaningful when the religious man is not ready in any situation to allow his statements being falsified. But there is no such difficulty of understanding and no communication gap between all those who by sharing a common attitude undergo the same or similar kind of vision which has a perfectly objective depth and a cognitive status. Because they all face a momentous objective situation, it is quite natural for them to make factual or cognitive statements, the deeper meaning of which they all understand and communicate amongst themselves. The situation although not objective and factual in the ordinary sense is still objective and factual in its own unique sense.

We have so far been driving at the point that the logic of the word 'God' is the same as the logic of the word 'Beauty'. But there is an essential difference between the two. We have seen that religion is a matter of ultimate concern and therefore the situation in which the religious man experiences God in the world is momentously different from the situation in which the man experiences beauty in an object. The latter is a case coming under the range of our ordinary concerns of daily life, but the former is a case with which the questions of our existence or life and death are associated. It concerns the man in a very deep and significant way. The man is totally involved in the situation with his total personality. The discovery or discernment is made here by what the existentialists would call being-in-the situation. The cause which is at stake here is very crucial and significant. And therefore the discernment situation in which man discovers a God in the universe cannot really be compared fully to any other situation. In it the man is really 'convicted' or 'overpowered' by the discernment. His total life is changed thereby. His impression is a total impression. All his feelings, thought and action now get a new orientation. He now discerns a new light in the universe and that has an epoch-making and far-reaching consequence upon his total life. The momentous disclosure makes the man a totally changed man now. He becomes fully committed to a specific way of life in all its aspects-in feeling, thought and action. This is why Ramsey characterises such a situation as 'discernment-commitment' situation.[10] All these amply go to show why the religious man is not ready to take his belief falsified in any conceivable situation. The momentous disclosure which involves the total personality of the man shakes him from the very foundation and takes hold of him. Naturally, he is never ready to allow anything to count against his vision and belief.

We have seen above why the religious man does not allow his belief being falsified in any situation and still has reasons to express his belief in the factual or cognitive form. The factual form of the religious belief finds its further vindication in the act of symbolisation which is a necessary part or aspect of the religious situation. We have seen that it is in the situation of being ultimately concerned that man discerns the dimension of divinity in the universe. It is quite natural, therefore, that after the discernment, man may feel tempted or rather constrained (due to the seriousness of the concern) to establish a living relationship with his God. But it is very difficult to establish such a relation with an abstract reality. The divine so far in its all-pervading status is more or less an abstract something with which man finds himself unable to establish a relation. He therefore, begins to employ symbols, so that the abstract reality may be concretized somehow. Symbols are perhaps the best media for realising or concretizing an abstraction. This is why symbolisation is so important in religion. Tillich has pointed out very significantly in his book *Dynamics of Faith* that symbols point beyond themselves and participate in the reality of the object which they symbolise.[11] Thus for example, the flag of a nation serves as a symbol of the nation. The flag as the symbol of the nation points beyond itself in the sense that its significance is no longer confined to its being a piece of coloured cloth, rather it points much beyond that insignificant character of its own. It has a sense of sacredness, a sense of dignity and honour around it. It stands for something very great which is much beyond its actual physical existence. But then it also participates in the reality, the existence of the nation which it symbolises. The nation in itself proves to be something abstract and therefore one is hardly able to pay his love and affection and honour towards his nation quite directly. It is through the flag of the nation that the individual finds himself more concretely associated with the soul of his nation and in the symbol of the flag he finds a medium for his sentiments towards his nation to find a concrete shape. In a similar fashion man wants a symbol which goes beyond itself and participates in the reality of the discernment that he makes in the universe. God as ordinarily understood in the personal form amply serves to act as such a symbol. Through the symbol of God man becomes able to establish a living relation with the abstract discernment that he has made. He also becomes able through that symbol to give concrete and practical shape to his various feelings by performing various religious acts directed towards the symbol. God proves to be a medium for establishing a lively bond between the religious man and the new all-pervasive reality that he discerns in the universe.

God is, as Tillich says, the primary religious symbol. Through this symbol man tries to establish a living meaningful relationship with the reality that he finds present throughout the universe. But there are other secondary religious symbols also which play their roles in religion. Such secondary symbols are mostly constituted by such mythical personalities as Ram, Krishna, Jehovah etc. Around such personalities several mythical stories are found and they constitute a very significant part of the religion in which they flourish. Braithwaite, we have seen, has very ably pointed to the significance of such stories in the sphere of religion. These myths and symbols enable the religious man to establish a living communion with his deity. Altizer has said about myths that they are "the symbolic representations of faith"[12] Again, about their necessary significance in religion he says. "We are forced to employ myths and symbol at precisely those points where our (ordinary) ideas and concepts break down."[13] We have seen that the unique discernment really casts a fascinating impression upon the religious man and his ordinary ideas and concepts really break down. Myths and their symbols in a way come to the rescue of the fascinated man. It is by employing myths and symbols that he gives his experience a concrete shape and makes able to express his deep feelings towards that in some tangible ways. Moreover, these myths and symbols give man an opportunity for a continual representation of his experience and some- times help him also in inducing such experiences again and again. As Altizer very ably notes, "Whenever man has an experience of the sacred, he symbolises it by means of myth and thus makes possible its continual representation."[14] These symbols again make religion a social phenomenon. In other words, it is through these religious symbols and myths that the whole society participates in the reality of a single deity and the members are tried up in a common bond of religious unity. The religious symbol sometimes becomes a symbol of social unity and the members unite together in several kinds of social, religious and sacramental bonds. Such communal or social participations in a deity symbolised by a particular symbol were more frequent in the primitive societies. In the totem animal, for example, the members of a particular class were tied up in a special social and religious bond. The totem animal, in other words, symbolised the deity of the whole society and through it the members were unified in a special bond. Even at present such social or communal participations in reality or God through special symbols are not rare. Hindu, Muslim, Christian and such other religious communities have all their participations in their God through special symbols of their own.

So far, we have tried to analyse the logic of the subject-term 'God' of God-statements. The question of the meaning of the word 'God' or of the status of the reality to which the word refers is, of course, the core of the question of the nature of theistic belief. But to make the nature of this belief still clearer it seems necessary to go into at least a brief analysis of the various predicates, such as, 'omnipotent', 'omniscient', benevolent' etc., associated with the subject term 'God'. We have seen that attempt at giving these predications a descriptive meaning have utterly failed. We must, therefore, have to look into the real import of these seemingly descriptive predicates associated with the term 'God'. And for that we will have to take hints from the logic of the subject term 'God' itself.

We have tried to show that the logic of the term 'God' is similar to that of the word 'Beauty'. In other words, the logic of seeing God in the universe is similar in nature to the logic of seeing beauty in an object. The statements about God, therefore, will be naturally similar in nature to the statements about beauty. But it is really very difficult to make statements about beauty. Beauty-experiences or experiences of the type of beauty are most primary and basic in nature and therefore it is very difficult to interpret, analyse or describe them in some other terms. Such experiences are to be felt from within, but it is very difficult to describe them in plain words. However, if the man experiencing beauty is asked to express his experience in words, he will have perhaps no other option than to use certain metaphors or exclamations for expressing the content of his experience. He will perhaps use such words, as 'Excellent', 'Lovely', 'Sweet' etc., but none of these words would have any descriptive import in that context. These words would simply reveal how deeply and in what an approbative way the man is affected by the experience he is having. Similarly, when one sees God in the universe, he has rather the most primary, basic and *sui genere's* experience. It is even more difficult than the beauty-experience to describe it in plain words. Beauty-situations are more than one and it may be possible in some sense to compare the experience of one situation with that of the other and express to some extent the nature of beauty. But God-experience is a unique experience, having no other parallel to it. Comparison in this case is rather impossible. This is why God-experience is said to be really indescribable and persons having such experience prefer to be silent. If any descriptions are thought to be possible, they are only in negative terms, *neti, neti,* as the Upanishads say. Thus the various predicates used in relation to God are not to be given any real descriptive value. They are attempts at somehow giving vent to the unique experience that the religious man has during his vision of a new dimension in the world-and-life situation as a whole. By using various predicates, the man does not really describe the objective situation (because a description in this case is not possible) he is facing. He is rather somehow trying to give vent to the uniquely deep, intense and fascinating experience that he is having. His words are really the words of exclamation and approbation.

Due to his being most deeply convicted by the situation of God-discernment, he wants to express that in such terms which convey meanings even far greater than what superlatives can do. As he has no other way out but to use ordinary predicate-words, he begins to add certain prefixed like 'omni' or certain adverbs like 'infinitely', 'necessarily' etc. to them to express the intensity of his sense. Thus the predicate-words used in relation to 'God' do not express literal descriptive meaning. They actually express the sense of uniqueness with which the man is fascinated, overwhelmed and overpowered by the discernment he has made in the universe. The predicates are all exclamatory, approbative and evaluative in import.

But there is a sense in which the predicates may be regarded as descriptive too. We have seen that the religious man after having the unique discernment tries to concretize it by means of certain symbols. The symbols, thus, make the discernment somewhat concretely objective. The symbol of personal God is the most effective, and the somewhat descriptive character of the various predicates can be seen in relation to this God-symbol. In other words, we can say that the various predications of God in a way form part of the same effort at concretisation of the otherwise formless nature of the original vision.

In relation to the concretised symbol, the predicates somehow assume a descriptive character, but not purely literally. They do so rather somewhat metaphorically. However, in their true nature, the predicates are only exclamatory and evaluative and not descriptive. Their descriptiveness is only secondary and can be understood only in relation to the symbolised form of the original vision. It must, however, to kept in mind that symbols are only media of participation in the formless reality, they are by themselves not that reality. Thus the descriptive nature of the predicates in relation to these symbols does not represent their true nature. In their true nature, they are hardly descriptive.

We have so far tried to analyse the true nature of theistic belief in the light of some of the typical assertions made by the theistic believer. We have tried to do justice to both the important features exhibited by the religious man's assertion of his belief, i.e. his assertion of it with a full factual force and at the same time his sticking to it with a sense of commitment such that he would never allow it to be falsified. We have, in other words, tried to find a logic behind the theistic statements. being factual and non-falsifiable both at the same time. And to our mind, as we have asserted earlier, also, any analysis of religious belief or statements must do justice to both of these features. Attempts at analysing theistic statements as perfectly factual more or less in the ordinary sense by totally ignoring their non-falsifiable character (or by mistakenly proving their falsifiability) are as one-sided as those taking them as simply non-falsifiable (and hence in consequence as purely emotive, or purely conative etc.) by totally ignoring their factual form. Theistic statements are in a sense factual, as we have seen, but the speciality and the distinction of the factual nature must be clearly understood. Similarly, they can, in a sense, be called emotive, because various kinds of feelings and emotions are surely associated with the grand unique discernment that the religious man makes in the universe. It is these feelings and emotions associated with the vision, which find expression through the various metaphysical and ethical attributes that the religious man assigns to the object of his vision. They also find expression through the various kinds of behaviour that he makes in relation to his object of vision, mostly after giving it a concrete form through acts of symbolisation. Thus religious statements are emotive in the sense that some of very intense feelings and emotions of the religious man are associated with the object of his vision, when the man undergoes the unique type of experience in relation to the universe as a whole. They are not emotive in that pejorative sense which seems characteristic of the view of some of the logical positivists like A.J. Ayer. Religious statements are not emotive in the sense that they mean simply being engrossed in certain purely subjective feelings, emotions or passions which might prove to be a subject-matter, as Ayer says, only for a psycho-analyst. Even if there are certain feelings or emotions associated with religious belief or beliefs, as there really are, they have behind them a uniquely objective base of experience.

In a similar way, again, it can be seen that characterising religious statements as conative, or, as Braithwaite would say, as statements expressing intention or will to lead a specific way of life, is not wholly out of place; it is only partial and one-sided. We have said that when the religious man discerns the new dimension in the universe in his unique experience, it has a very deep and far-reaching impact on his life and his whole life-pattern undergoes a radical transformation in its light. A specific way of behaviour or life-pattern therefore is necessarily associated with the religious belief and hence morality constitutes a very important aspect of every religion. But that cannot be regarded as the very essence of religion. That does not constitute the central core of religion, Hare seems to be very correct when he writes: "the moral judgments ... arise out of religious belief; they do not constitute it."[15] Thus religious belief is not constituted by moral ideas or beliefs, rather the latter are the inevitable consequences of the former. The vision which is at the root of religious belief naturally issues forth in a set of moral ideas and beliefs and leads to a specific way of life. Thus Braithwaite and others, as we have said earlier also, do not seem to be correct in analysing religious belief to be identical in essence with moral belief. Religious belief differs from moral belief not only in the point that while the former is associated with certain myths and stories, the latter is not. The difference is rather much too deeper. Religion or religious belief has its primary essence in the unique vision of an all-pervasive reality in the universe which is later on symbolised as God. The moral way of life is just the consequence of this vision. Religious statements are primarily ontological statements referring to objective situation, although certain moral beliefs become naturally associated with them.

A similar error has been committed more recently by one J.G. Wilson in course of his analysis of Samkar's advaitic statements. Drawing indirectly upon recent analysis like Braithwaite, he tries to re-interpret Samkar's statements as moral recommendations or as talks of value and commitment to a certain type of moral behaviour.

The seeming ontological implications of Samkar's statements are, according to him, misleading. Therefore "We have to transpose his metaphysical terminology into talk of values and commitment to moral behaviour which retains the peculiarities of language without the misleading metaphysical implications."[16] To illustrate his point Wilson interprets the advaitic statement 'thou art that' (*Tat Tvam Asi*) as "the recommendation as to how you should value your neighbour and therefore behave towards him."[17] But Wilson, like Braithwaite, forgets here that although a moral recommendation of the nature of 'you should behave towards your neighbour in a specific way' is associated with or arises out of the belief 'Thou art that', that does not constitute its essential meaning. The primary use of such advaitic statements is ontological, although quite naturally a true understanding of the ontological meaning of such statements leads to a specific way of moral life. The statement 'thou art that' primarily refers to a unique kind of ontological experience in which the basic reality appears to be a non-dual unity. From Samkar's report of the ontological experience that the world is basically a complete spiritual unity, that there. is absolutely no distinction between oneself and another, and that between the self (thou) and the *Brahman* (that) there is a complete identity, one may very well derive the moral that one should value one's neighbour as one's own self, but that is not the primary meaning of the statement 'thou art that'. In its primary import, the statement refers to a unique experience which is in no way comparable to ordinary fact-experience. The statement is certainly not an ordinary proposition, but still it has a referential import of a unique kind. All the different advaitic statements of Samkara are the expressions of the same basic experience which finds the whole universe somehow uniquely enveloped, pervaded, permeated and dwelt in by a reality which eludes all our ordinary grasp and apprehension. The universe in that unique experience looks to Samkara as. undivided unity, and that is what he expresses through his various advaitic statements. From such an experience, the inevitable moral no doubt follows that gross egoism is illusory and misconceived and one should treat everyone as his own being.

But that is not the main import of Samkar's statement. The main import is ontological. Hence, religious statements cannot be taken as essentially and exhaustively moral in character. Basically they refer to an ontological experience which is uniquely objective in its nature and specific moral beliefs and a specific way of life follow as a consequence of that unique vision or experience.

## REFERENCES

1. R.B. Braithwaite, op. cit., p. 15.
2. John Hick, Faith and Knowledge, pp. 127-28

3. Paul Tillich, Systematic Theology, Vol. I, p. 17.

4. Ibid., pp. 17 ff.

5. W.F. Zuurdeeg, op. cit., p. 28.

6. John Hick, op. cit., 120-25.

7. Ibid., Introduction, p. xii.

8. W.F. Zuurdeeg, op. cit., p. 53.

9. John Wisdom, 'Gods in A. Flew's Logic and Language, Ist. Series, p. 192.

10. I.T. Ramsey, Religious Language, pp. 15ff.

11. Paul Tillich, Dynamics of Faith, p. 42. Also Systematic Theology (Vol.I), p. 239.

12. T.J.J. Altizer, 'The Religious meaning of Myth and Symbol' included in T.J.J. Altizer etc. (ed.) Truth, Myth, and Symbol, p. 95.

13. Ibid., p. 90.

14. Ibid., p. 96.

15. R.M. Hare, 'Religion and Morals' included in B. Mitchell's (ed.) Faith and Logic, p. 179.

16. J.G. Wilson, Sankara, Ramanuja and the Function of Religious Language' in Religious Studies (March, 1970), p. 66.

17. Ibid.

# 6
# CONCLUDING OBSERVATIONS

We have does tried in our previous pages to make a thorough going survey of the contemporary situation in philosophical theology, specially with regard to the nature of religious statements and through them of religious belief and in the end have tried to take a position of our own in this regard which we think amply justifies the rationale behind the two obviously contradictory ways in which the religious believers utter their religious statements. But on the basis of the survey and the position taken by us, three observations may be made which are according to us very important and striking. We shall take them up below one by one:

1. The religious statements, more particularly the theistic statements refer to an impression or experience which is pantheistic in nature rather than theistic. In their words the original impression is pantheist or pantheist and the thorough expression in the form of three sticky statements are the result of some lame manipulations more probably of the act of symbolisation. The distinction between pantheism (or panentheism) and theism, therefore, seems to be a matter of stages. The same experience which at its basic stage is pantheistic in nature becomes theistic at a later stage by some act or acts of human expediency. This remainds of the shankara vedantic position where the basic reality is explained or envisioned as an attributeless

nirakar Brahmn, and for human convenience of establishing a concrete relationship of devotion praise etc. It is converted into a God full of attributes. Does the place where we finally reach by an analysis of artistic statements is in a way recognition of Shankar's position bringing about a distinction between Brahmn and God (Ishwara). The same experience which adds its basic or original stage is pantheistic or panentheistic in nature becomes theistic at a later stage. Shankar's distinction between Brahma and Ishwar, it seems to us, is a recognition of this truth. Though basically all is according to him Brahma, God is a very useful symbol of Brahma in as much as it serves as a medium through which the ordinary man establish his relation with nirankar Brahmn or participate in the reality of Brahma. However it has to be kept in mind that what is ultimate is Brahma and God is a symbol through which man satisfy all his religious aspirations. The truth is testified in the views of Paul Tillich also when he takes the basic reality as being and God is a mere symbol of this basic reality. However if someone wants to take God himself as the highest or basic reality, he will have to characterise God as being itself. All other theistic statements are merely symbolic in nature.

2. Although religion has been more basic and important in human life then many things else including philosophising, but still the most problematic issue for philosophy of religion has been to advance an adequate definition of religion which envelopes all the prevailing religions of the world within its fold, or in other words, which equally applies to all the religions of the world. But if we go seriously and closely through our analysis of religious statements in our previous pages by virtue of which we have been able to reach a position regarding the nature of religious belief, we believe that we will find such a definition of religion which will satisfy the condition of adequacy that we have laid down above.

We have seen that religious belief is a product of some strong impression or a vision with regard to the universe as a whole and the vision mesmerise or overpower the man having the vision that he adopts a whole way of life in a pervasive manner in the light of that vision.

In the light of the purely conative analyses of religious belief, religion is sometimes defined, as it has actually been done by Paul Schmidt, as a way of life. The phrase 'way of life', however, is given a wide meaning and it is said that it denotes not only actual external behaviour, but also internal feelings and thoughts. To be religious therefore means to feel, think and behave in a specific way. Religion is, thus, as it is said, a pervasive way of life, which includes both internal and external behaviour. The above definition of religion cannot be taken as wrong but it is only partially correct, i.e. it expresses only a part of the full nature of religion. Religion, as understood in its practical aspect, is of course a way of life, a pervasive way of life, as it has been said. The distinction between a man who is religious and one who is not religious can be brought about, at least on the practical level, by seeing what type of life the one leads in contrast with the other, i.e., how he feels, thinks, speaks and behaves in contrast with the other. When Gandhi was asked as to what his religion was, he replied: "You must watch my life, how I live, eat, sit, talk, behave in general. The sum-total of all those in me is my religion."[1] Thus religion is certainly a way of life. But the way of life which is characteristic of the practical aspect of religion is not rootless. Our analysis so far, if understood in its true spirit, amply shows that behind the way of life pervasively adopted, there is a vision, an experience, a strong impression on the part of the religious man in relation to the universe as a whole. It is this vision or strong impression that the man has in relation to the universe as a whole, that gives him a specific way of life. "Vision and action go together", says Radhakrishnan.[2] Being convicted by the unique discernment that the religious man makes in the universe as a whole, he adopts a specific way of life, a specific pattern of behaviour, inner and outer. *In the light of these truth related to the nature of religious belief, we must define religion as way of life based on a strong conviction with regard to the universe or world-and-life as a whole.* The latter part of the definition is as much important (rather in certain respects even more important) as the former. Here the phrase strong conviction' must be understood in all its implications that we have tried to render clear in course of our analysis of the true nature of religious belief.

But if religion is defined in the above way, we will have to realise that atheism would be as much religious in nature as theism is taken to be. We have seen that both theism and atheism are the results of being very strongly impressed or convicted by the same universe in two different ways. So if one is regarded as religious, the other also must be taken as such. What, however, is required is that atheistic belief also must give rise to a specific way of life. If someone adopts a pervasive way of life in strict conformity and consistency with his atheistic belief he must be regarded as much religious in character as a theistic believer is taken to be by virtue of his adoption of a specific way of life in the light of his theistic conviction and belief. Religion, we have said, is a way of life, a pervasive way of life, based on a strong conviction with regard to the universe as a whole. Theism and atheism both are the outcomes of two different convictions of the same level with regard to the universe as a whole, and therefore both must be regarded equally well as religious in character, provided both of them give rise to two different ways of life in conformity with their respective characters. If an atheist lives firmly up to his atheistic conviction, he is as much religious as a loyal theist is. In point of logic there seems to be no reason why one is to be taken as religious and the other is not.

We have seen above that at least in point of logic, both theism and atheism may equally be regarded as religious in character. Theistic belief and practices may be taken to constitute one specific kind of religion, while atheistic belief and practices may be taken as constituting a religion of another specific kind. But here it may be seen that atheism itself is of two kinds. There is one kind of atheism which not only disbelieves in the existence of God, but also disbelieves in the existence of any supramundane, transcendental or spiritual values or goal. Gross materialism is the example of such an atheism. There may be an atheistic religion in this sense also in as much as there may be persons who have out and out materialistic conviction in regard to world and life and who live a life strictly loyal to such a conviction. But there is another kind of atheism, which, of course, does not believe in God, but still believes in the reality of certain extramundane and spiritual values and goal. According to this kind of atheism although there is no God behind the world, still the material world and the present life are not ultimate. There is a realm of spiritual values and there is a spiritual goal to be attained by man as his highest end. Buddhism and Jainism may be taken as examples of this kind of atheistic religion. However, what is important to note is that in both these forms of atheistic religion, there is a specific conviction with regard to world-and-life as a whole and there is a specific way of life in tune with that conviction.

On our analysis of the nature of religion, theism and atheism have equally come to be religious provided they give rise to the respective ways of life commensurate with them. But traditionally, at least atheism of the gross materialistic type has not been regarded as religion. On the other hand, again, theism alone has also not been recognised as religion. Buddhism and Jainism even in spite of being atheistic in their essential character have been universally recognised as religious. Thus, in the traditional concept what has distinguished religion from irreligion is not the element of belief in God, but what may be called a spiritualistic conviction in regard to world and life as a whole on the part of the former. If we like therefore to present a strictly descriptive definition of religion in the light of the prevalent religions, it will be something like the following : *Religion is a way of life based on a spiritualistic conviction towards world-and-life as a whole.* The spiritualistic conviction itself is a specific type of conviction and that way the present definition comes within the scope of the definition that we have advanced earlier. The word 'spiritualistic' may be troublesome and it may need clarification. But assuming that there is no trouble at least in regard to a general sense that it carries with it, we are not going here in the details of its clarification.

At last it can be seen that we have been able to arrive at our definition of religion by an analysis of the theistic statements in general, but the definition as much applies to the non-theistic or atheistic religions as it applies to theistic religions. Believing that there is a God behind the world and he is the creator, sustainer, etc. of this world represents one kind of specific conviction in regard to the world-and-life situation as a whole and believing that there is no God as the creator etc., but the world-and-life situation has a spiritualistic foundation and that the goal of human life is spiritual represent another kind of specific conviction with regard to the world-and-life situation as a whole. There are ways of life attached to both the convictions or impressions and hence both are equally religious in character.

3. It can be seen from the above that although the way of life does not constitute all-in-all of religion and religion cannot be defined solely in terms of a way of life,

still the fact that religion is a way of life is very important in one respect. It is really this. aspect of religion which distinguishes it from metaphysics. On the manifest level, metaphysics of course seems to be a rational attempt to understand the nature of the universe as a whole.

But behind every true metaphysics there is involved strong impression or an overall vision regarding the universe on the; part of the metaphysician.

Indian metaphysics is basically and primarily a fruit of *darsana*. Once the metaphysician has this *darsana* regarding the nature of the universe as a whole, he tries to theorise it by means of his logic and reasoning. Thus true metaphysics and religion both have behind them as their basic root a strong impression, a vision in relation to the universe as a whole. The difference lies in the fact that whereas the metaphysician after having his vision engages himself in a rational theory-construction, the religious man engages himself in orienting his life in the light of that. Thus whereas religion becomes a way of life, metaphysics remains only on the level of understanding the nature of the world and life. In the light of the distinction so often brought about, between 'believing-in' and 'believing that' it can be said, that whereas religion is an example of 'believing-in', metaphysics is an example of 'believing that'. In other words it can be said that whereas religion is an outcome of man's serious concern regarding his life and existence, metaphysics is the outcome of a mere interest on the part of the metaphysician to understand world and life in their basic nature.

## REFERENCES

1. M.K. Gandhi, Harijan, Sept. 1946.

2. S. Radhakrishnan, *Eastern Religions and Western Thought*, p. 80.

# BIBLIOGRAPHY

Ayer, A.J., Language, Truth and Logic (London, Victor Gollanez, 1946).

Ayer, A.J., Demonstration of the Impossibility of Metaphysics' in Logical Positivism (New York, The Free Press of Glancoe, 1959), edited by A.J. Ayer.

Ayer, A.J., Logical Positivism-A Debate' (with Copleston) in A Modern Introduction to Philosophy (The Free Press of Glancoe, 1957), edited by Paul Edwards and A. Pap.

Aitizer, T.J.J., "The Religious Meaning of Myth and Symbol' in Truth, Myth and Symbol (Prentice Hall, 1962), edited by T.J.J. Altizer, William A. Beardslee and J. Harvey Young.

Austin, John, 'Performative Utterances' in Philosophical Papers (London, Oxford University Press, 1961), a collection of articles by Austin and published posthumously.

Austin, John, 'Other Minds' in Logic and Language, Second Series (Oxford, Basil Blackwell, 1953), edited by A.G.N. Flew.

Allen, R.E., 'The Ontological Argument' in Philosophical Review, January 1961.

Abelson, R., 'Not Necessarily' in Philosophical Review, January 1961.

Alston, F.P., The Ontological Argument Revisited' in Philosophical Review, Vol. 69, 1960.

Alston, F.P., "Meaning and Use' in Philosophical Quarterly, Vol. 62, 1963.

Blanshard, B., Reason and Analysis (London, Allen & Unwin, 1962).

Braithwaite, R.B., An Empiricist's View of the Nature of Religious Belief (Cambridge University Press, 1955).

Blackstone, W.T., The Problem of Religious Knowledge (Prentice Hall, 1963).

Ballie, John, The Sense of the Presence of God (Oxford University Press, 1962).

Brown, Patterson, 'Religious Morality' in Mind, April 1963.

Campbell, K., 'Patterson Brown on God and Evil' in Mind, October 1965.

Crombie, I.M., "Theology and Falsification' in New Essays in Philosophical Theology (New York, Macmillan, 1955), S.C.M., cheap ed., 1963), edited by A. Flew and A. MacIntyre.

Crombie, I.M., "The Possibility of Theological Statements' in Faith and Logic (London, Allen & Unwin, 1957), edited by B. Mitchell.

Carnap, R., "Truth and Confirmation' in Readings in Philosophical Analysis (New York, Appleton-Century Crofts, 1949), edited by H. Feigl and W. Sellars.

Carnap, R., Testability and Meaning' in Philosophy of Science, Vol. III (1936), and Vol. IV (1937).

Carnap, R., Elimination of Metaphysics through a Logical Analysis of Language' in Logical Positivism, edited by A.J. Ayer.

# BIBLIOGRAPHY

Carnap, R., Philosophy and Logical Syntax (London, Routledge & Kegan Paul, 1935).

Duff-Forbes, D.R., "Theology and Falsification Again' in Australasian Journal of Philosophy, August 1961.

Eliade, Mercia, Myth and Reality (George Allen & Unwin, Copyright-Harper & Row, New York, 1963).

Ewing, A.C., 'Awareness of God' in Philosophy, January 1965.

Edwards, Paul, 'Prof. Tillich's Confusion' in Mind, April 1965.

Edwards, Paul, 'Some Notes on Anthropomorphic Theology' in On Religious Experience and Truth (Oliver & Boyed, 1962, New York, University Press, 1961), edited by Sydney Hook.

Feigl, Herbert, 'Logical Empiricism' in Twentieth Century Philosophy (New York, Philosophical Library, 1943), edited by D.D. Runes.

Feigl, Herbert, 'Empiricism Vs. Theolgy' in A Modern Introduction to Philosophy, edited by Paul Edwards & A. Pap.

Ferre, F., Language, Logic and God (London, Eyre & Spothswoode, 1961-62).

Foster, Michael, " 'We' in Modern Philosophy" in Faith and Logic, edited by B. Mitchell.

Findlay, J.N., 'Can God's Existence be Disproved ?' in A. Flew's (ed.) New Essays in Philosophical Theology.

Flew, A.G.N., 'Theology and Falsification' in New Essays in Philosophical Theology.

Flew, A.G.N., 'Divine Omnipotence and Human Freedom' in New Essays in Philosophical Theology.

Flew, A. G.N., "The Religous Morality' of Patterson Brown" in Mind, October 1965.

Flew, A.G.N., "Creation' in New Essays in Philosophical Theology.

Flew, A.G.N., 'The Justification of Punishment', Philsophy,1954.

Franklin, R.L., Necessary Being' in Australasian Journal of Philosophy, August 1957.

Gandhi, M.K., Harijan, Sept. 1946.

Gibson, A. Boyce, 'Modern Philosophers Consider Religion' in Australasian Journal of Philosophy, Vol. 35, No. 3.

Hartshorne, Charles, "The Logic of Perfection' in Hick's & Megill's (ed.) The Many Faced Argument.

Hempel, Karl G., 'Empiricist Criterion of Meaning' in Logical Positivism, edited by A.J. Ayer.

Hempel, Karl G., "The Concept of Cognitive Significance' in Proceedings of the American Academy of Arts and Science, Vol. 80, 1951.

Hick, John, Faith and Knowledge (Ithaca, Cornell University Press, 1957).

Hick, John, 'Meaning and Truth in Religion' in Religious Experience and Truth, edited by Sydney Hook.

Hick, John, 'Sceptics and Believers' in Faith and Philosophers (London, Macmillan, 1964), edited by John Hick.

Hick, John, 'Theology and Verification' in The Existence oj God (New York, Macmillan, 1964), edited by John Hick.

Hospers, John, An Introduction to Philosophical Analysis (Prentice Hall, Englewood Cliffs, 1953).

Hepburn, R.W., Christianity and Paradox (C.A. Watts & Co., London, 1958).

Hepburn, R.W., From World to God' in Mind, January 1963.

Hutchings, P.A.E., Necessary Being and Some Types of Tautology' in Philosophy, January 1964.

Hare, R.M., "Theology and Falsification' in New Essays in Philosophical Theology.

Hare, R.M., 'Religion and Morals' in Faith & Logic, edited by B. Mitchell.

Henelle, Paul, "Uses of Ontological Argument' in Philosophical Review, January 1961.

Hughes, G.E., Can God's Existence be Disproved?' in Now Essays in Philosophical Theology.

Hayner, Paul, 'Analogical Predication' in Journal of Philosophy, September 1958.

Hume, David, Dialogues Concerning Natural Religion.

Hume, David, An Essay Concerning Human Understanding. Kant, I., Critique of Pure Reason, Eng. Tr. by N.K. Smith.

Kneale, W.F., 'Is Existence a Predicate?' in New Essays in Philosophical Analysis, edited by Feigl & Sellars.

Keirkegaard, S., "The Absolute Paradox' in The Existence of God, edited by John Hick.

Kaufmann, W., Critique of Religion and Philosophy (Faber & Faber, London, 1958).

Kennick, W.E., "The Language of Religion' in Philosophical Review, Vol. 65, 1956.

Lewis, H.D., Our Experiences of God (London, Allen & Unwin 1959).

Lewis, H.D., 'Recent Empiricism and Religion' in Philosophy, July, 1957.

Lewis, H.D., 'The Cognitive Factor in Religious Experience', Proceedings of the Aristotelian Society, Vol. XXIX

Lewis, H.D., "God and Mystery' in Prospect for Metaphysics, edited by Tan Ramsey.

Lazerowitz, M., "The Positivist Use of Nonsense' in The Structure of Metaphysics (London, Routledge and Kegan Paul, 1955).

Martin, C.., 'A Religious Way of Knowing' in New Essays in Philosophical Theology.

Martin, C.B., "The Perfect Good' in A. Flew's (ed.) New Eassys in Philosophical Theology.

Martin, C.B., Religious Belief (N.Y., Cornell University Press, 1959).

Mace, C.A., 'Representation & Expression' in Philosophy and Analysis (Basil Blackwell, Oxford, 1954), edited by M. Macdonald.

MacIntyre, A.C., Difficulties in Christian Belief (London, S.C.M., 1959).

Macintyre, A.C., 'The Logical Status of Religious Belief' in Metaphysical Belief (London, S.C.M., 1957), edited by

A. MacIntyre & R.G. Smith. Mascall, E.L., 'Is Theological Discourse Possible' included in Philosophy of Religion (New York, Macmillan, 1962), edited by Abernethy & Langford.

Mascall, E.L., "The Doctrine of Analogy' in Philosophy of Religion, edited by Abernethy & Langford.

McPherson, T., "Assertion & Analogy' in Proceeding of the Aristotelian Society, Vol. 60, 1959-60.

Milmed, Bella, K., "Theories of Religious Knowledge from Kant to Jaspers' in Philosophy, Vol. 29, 1954.

Miles, T.R., Religion & Scientific Outlook (George Allen & Unwin, London, 1959).

Mises, Richard Von, Positivism (Oxford University Press, 1951).

Mitchell, B., 'Theology & Falsification' in A. Flew's (ed.) New Essays in Philosophical Theology.

Mitchell, B., "The Grace of God' in Faith & Logic, edited by B. Mitchell.

Mitchell, B., "The Justification of Religious Belief' in Philosophical Quarterly, July 1961.

Moore, G.E., Is Existence a Predicate ?' in A. Flew's (ed.) Logic and Language, Second Series (Basil Blackwell, 1953).

Malcolm, N., 'Anselm's Ontological Argument' in Fhilosophical Review, Vol. 69, 1960.

Mackie, J.L., Evil & Omnipotence' in Mind, Vol. LXIV, 1955.

Mill, J.S., Three Essays on Religion.

Neilson, Kai, 'Eschatological Verification' in Abernethy etc. (ed.) Philosophy of Religion.

Nowell-Smith, P.H., Ethics (London, 1954).

Pap, A., Elements of Analytic Philosophy (New York, Macmillan, 1949).

Passmore, John, 'Logical Positivism' in The Australasian Journal of Philosophy, Vol. 21, 1943.

Plantinga, A., 'A Valid Ontological Argument?' in Philosophical Review, January 1961.

Penelhum, T., 'Divine Necessity' in Mind, April 1960.

Penelhum, T., 'On the Second Ontological Argument' in Philosophical Review, January 1961.

Puccetti, R., 'Is Omniscience Possible ?' in Australasian Journal of Philosophy, May 1963.

Puccetti, R., 'The Concept of God' in Philosophical Quarterly July 1964.

Platt, David, 'God, Goodness and Morally Perfect World' in The Personalist, Summer 1965.

Popper, Karl, The Logic of Scientific Discovery (New Basic Books, Inc., 1959).

Popper, Karl, Conjectures and Refutations (New York, Basic Books, 1963).

Radhakrishnan, S., Eastern Religions and Western Thought (Oxford Univ. Press, 1939).

Ramsey, I.T., Religious Language (S.C.M., London, 1957).

Root, Howard, Metaphysics and Religious Belief' in Prospect for Metaphysics (New York, Philosophical Library, 1961), edited by Ian T. Ramsey.

Rainer, A.C.A., 'Can God's Existence be Disproved?' in A. Flew's (ed.) New Essays in Philosophical Theology.

Reichenbach, H., The Rise of Scientific Philosophy (University of California Press, 1951).

Ross, J.F., 'God and "Logical Necessity"' in Philosophical Quarterly, January 1961.

Ruja, Harry, "The Ontological Argument and a 'Living Faith'" in The Personalist, Summer 1963.

Russell, B., "A Debate on the Existence of God' (with Copleston) in John Hick's (ed.) 'The Existence of God'.

Russell, B., Logic and Knowledge (George Allen & Unwin, 1964).

Ryle, G., "The Theory of Meaning' in British Philosophy in the Mid-Century (London, Allen & Unwin, 1957), edited by C.A. Mace.

Ryle, G., The Concept of Mind (London, Hutchinson & Co., 1949).

Ryle, G., 'Systematically Misleading Expressions' in Logic and Language, First Series (Basil Blackwell, 1951), edited by A. Flew.

Ryle, G., "Ordinary Language' in Philosophical Review, Vol. 62, 1953.

Schlick, M., "Meaning & Verification' in Readings in Twentieth Century Philosophy (The Free Press of Glancoe, 1963), edited by F.P. Alston & George Nakhnikian.

Schlick, M., Positivism & Realism' in Logical Positivism, edited by A.J. Ayer.

Strawson, P.F., "Truth' in Analysis, June 1949.

Strawson, P.F., An Introduction to Logical Theory (London, Mathuen & Co., 1952).

Strawson, P.F., 'On Referring' in Essays in Conceptual Analysis (New York, St. Martin's Press, 1956), edited by A. Flew.

Stevenson, Charles, 'Persuasive Definitions' in Mind, Vol. 47, 1938.

Smith, John E., Reason and God (New Haven & London : Yale University Press, 1961).

Smart, J.J.C., 'The Existence of God' in A. Flew's (ed.) New Essays in Philosophical Theology.

Smart, Ninian, Reasons and Faiths (Routledge and Kegan Paul,: 1958).

Shaffer, J., 'Existence, Predication and the Ontological Argument' in Mind, July 1962.

Schmidt, Paul F., Religious Knowledge Free Press of Glancoe, 1961).

Tennant, F.R., Philosophical Theology (Cambridge University Press, 1928-30).

Tillich, Paul, Dynamics of Faith (London, Allen & Unwin, 1957).

Tillich, Paul, Systematic Theology, Vol. I (The University of Chicago Press, 1961).

Urmson, J.O., Philosophical Analysis: Its Development between Two World Wars (New York, Oxford University Press, 1956).

Wittgenstein, L., Tractatus Logico-Philosophicus (London, Routledge and Kegan Paul, 1961), Eng. Tr. by D.F. Pears and B.F. McGuiness.

Wittgenstein, L., Philosophical Investigations (Oxford, Basil Blackwell, 1953), Eng. Tr. by G.E.M. Anscombe.

Wisdom, J.O., Metamorphosis of the Verifiability Theory of Meaning, in Mind, July 1963.

Wisdom, John, "Gods' in Logic and Language, First Series, edited by A. Flew.

Wisdom, John, 'Philosophical Perplexity' in Philosophy and Pschyo-Analysis (Oxford, Basil Blackwell, 1953).

Wisdom, John, 'Metaphysics & Verification' in Mind, Vol. 37, 1938.

Wisdom, John, Interpretation and Analysis (London, 1931).

Waisemann, F., "Verifiability' in A. Flew's (ed.) Logic and Language, First Series.

Waisemann, F., 'Language Strata' in Flew's (ed.) Logic and Language, Second Series.

Weitx, M., 'Oxford Philosophy' in Philosophical Review, Vol. 62, 1953.

Williams, C.J.F., God and "Logical Necessity" ' in Philosophical Quarterly, October 1961.

Wilson, John, Language and Christian Belief (London, Macmillan, 1958).

Wilson, John, Philosophy and Religion (London, Oxford University Press, 1961).

Wilson, J.G., Sankana, Ramanuja and the Function of Religious Language in Religions Studies, March 1970.

Wesley C. Salmon & George Nakhnikian, "'Exists' as a Predicate" in Philosophical Review, Vol. 66, 1957.

Zuurdeeg, W.F., An Analytic Philosophy of Religion (London, Allen & Unwin, 1959).